Sexual Offenders

Sexual Offenders explores and develops personal construct theory in terms of forensic and social psychology, and examines the possibilities for sexual offender assessment and therapy.

Rather than viewing sexual offenders as having a mental illness or possessing a set of pathological personality traits, personal construct theory indicates that all people learn particular ways of understanding their own experience, and use these "personal constructs" to anticipate the future. Through a variety of experiences, sexual offenders appear to develop a set of constructs that demands a particular understanding of themselves and other people. James Horley suggests that if they desire change sexual offenders can alter these constructs through psychotherapy. *Sexual Offenders* describes a number of techniques used by the author and other clinicians as well as presenting new and more dynamic approaches to psychological assessment.

Based on over 20 years of the author's clinical and research work, this book will provide professionals and students in the field of forensic psychology and psychiatry with an alternative way of treating sex offender clients.

Dr James Horley has worked with sexual offenders for more than 20 years in a variety of clinical settings, including prisons, forensic hospitals, and community agencies. He is the editor of *Personal Construct Perspectives on Forensic Psychology* (2003, Routledge). He is currently an associate professor of psychology at the University of Alberta in Camrose, Alberta, Canada.

Sexual Offenders

Personal construct theory and
deviant sexual behaviour

James Horley

Routledge
Taylor & Francis Group

LONDON AND NEW YORK

First published 2008
by Routledge
27 Church Road, Hove, East Sussex BN3 2FA

Simultaneously published in the USA and Canada
by Routledge
270 Madison Avenue, New York NY 10016

*Routledge is an imprint of the Taylor & Francis Group,
an Informa business*

© 2008 James Horley

Typeset in Times by
RefineCatch Limited, Bungay, Suffolk
Printed and bound in Great Britain by
TJ International Ltd, Padstow, Cornwall
Cover design by Design Deluxe, Bath, UK

This publication has been produced with paper manufactured to
strict environmental standards and with pulp derived from
sustainable forests.

British Library Cataloguing in Publication Data
A catalogue record for this book is available from the British Library

Library of Congress Cataloging-in-Publication Data
Horley, James, 1954–
   Sexual offenders : personal construct theory and deviant sexual
behaviour / James Horley.
      p. cm.
   Includes bibliographical references and index.
   1. Sex offenders—Psychology.   2. Sex offenders—
Rehabilitation.   3. Forensic psychology—Case studies.   I. Title.
HQ71.H67   2008
364.153—dc22   2007041892

ISBN: 978-1-58391-735-0

Contents

Figures

Preface

I have worked with criminal offenders for more than two decades and, although I now have other research interests and projects within psychology, I remain committed to forensic work in psychology. Much of my training and work in research and psychotherapeutics has focussed on sexual offenders, and exclusively male offenders. Reluctantly, I admit that I entered forensic work due to opportunities and income rather than more altruistic goals or intrinsic reasons. Quickly, however, after very few encounters with the men who would become my main client group, I discovered a number of compelling intellectual and ethical concerns that sparked and maintained my interest in criminal offenders in general and sexual offenders in particular.

Sexual offenders' lives and involvements provided puzzles that intrigued me. Why was it that, for example, a married, 42-year-old male who was a practicing heterosexual with three children would engage in sexual activities with a ten-year-old boy, a friend of his own son? Why would a mild-mannered university student, a bookworm from a wealthy family, stalk and assault a number of female classmates sexually? Why would a wealthy man with an apparently loving spouse regularly flash his genitals to young girls on a busy public street? As I met more clients, more questions arose, and this drew me further into a field that so many other mental health professionals left as quickly as they arrived, perhaps due to disgust with the clientele or frustration with the working conditions. Whatever led many service providers to abandon the business, I was more drawn to the field. At the same time, and perhaps part of the draw for me, the plight of many victims, including future victims, concerned me. These men who shared their troubled experiences showed me their potential for destruction, and I was worried. If someone does not provide clinical services, or attempts to get to the bottom of the behaviour of these offenders, either individually or collectively, how are we to prevent further victimization? Can we afford to ignore the issues, hoping that they will simply disappear over time? I became convinced that the issues surrounding sexual assault and abuse were real, serious, and required immediate attention. Too many women and children – indeed, men as well – had suffered already. Research into the causes of and solutions to inappropriate sexual behaviour is essential and long overdue.

Surprisingly, perhaps, I also began to feel some concern for the perpetrators of the sexual offenses themselves. I had to admit to myself that I did not find monsters: rather, I found men. Admittedly, in many cases, they were deeply troubled men who had caused untold suffering to their victims, their victims' families, and society in general, but they were men nonetheless. I discovered that many of them, likely only a minority but a sizeable one, seemed truly confused by their own acts, and they appeared to be honestly trying to change their ways. True, many of the offenders I met had no desire to alter their actions, and they appeared oblivious to the harm they had done, even taking some delight in the mayhem they had caused and the pain they had inflicted. These latter individuals, however, were not the overwhelming majority that I originally suspected.

If someone who has offended sexually against another asks for assistance, should help not be offered in the form of psychotherapy or some form of treatment? I soon decided that it certainly should. Fairly quickly after becoming a service provider at various correctional facilities in Canada I found that jails and prisons were not places for serious treatment of offenders, and I do not define the term "treatment" as simple incarceration like some more security-minded individuals do. Locking someone behind bars is treating the individual in some manner, but it is not treating them well if we confine the person to a grim setting where everyday, dog-eat-dog struggle for mere survival brutalizes the person more than any earlier brutality ever could.

Despite being on the virtual frontline of the battle, I was not sure what form any psychological intervention should take. Various reviews (e.g., Furby *et al.*, 1989) of therapy with sexual offenders were far from sanguine about the possibilities. With some relief and guarded optimism, I can now report that I have far more insight and understanding of sexual offenders gleaned from research, both my own and others, and my years of direct clinical experience. The purpose of this book is to share some of my experiences, insights, and lingering concerns, especially with those of you who are or hope to be in positions to influence how sexual offenders are treated. Quite intentionally, this book is not intended as a tome, a compendium of detailed information for only the most dedicated and specialized of those mental health professionals who work with sexual offenders. What I will present in this book succinctly is a radical departure from traditional conceptualization and psychotherapeutic treatment of sexual offenders. While I would not, and am not, advocating dispensing of all advances in terms of psychological assessment and psychotherapeutic technique employed with sexual offenders, I do argue that a new conceptual basis for continuing work with offenders is certainly required. I suggest a theoretical framework, Kelly's (1955) personal construct theory, that requires new directions in assessment and therapy. Some of the clinical strategies now considered as our "gold standards" may be tried, but they are far from true. My main point is that we need to consider new approaches in the psychological assessment and psychotherapy with sexual offenders, and I present and discuss a few possibilities that I think could prove valuable. Regardless of whether you are convinced by my arguments, my main goal in writing this book is to challenge you to expand your own theoretical, clinical, and personal boundaries. My hope is that you at least consider the development, use, and examination of varied and, ultimately, better approaches to assisting sexual offenders psychologically.

Acknowledgements

A number of theorists/clinicians/academics have contributed to my views to date, and they all deserve some mention. Some of their influences may have been inadvertent or indirect, but I would thank all equally. Probably the most important writer I have had the privilege to read is Professor George Kelly. Dr Kelly's irreverence, iconoclasm, and insights into the human condition have been among the most significant guiding forces in my professional life as a psychologist, to say nothing of my personal life. Kelly has spoken forcefully to me about how we as psychologists should proceed in understanding ourselves and other individuals, and how we should assist those who are in distress psychologically. Students of Kelly, especially Professors Jack Adams-Webber and Brian Little in Canada, have helped me to elaborate Kelly's ideas with correction and inspiration, and I appreciate the help of both over the years. Professor David Winter of England, a student of Kelly, has provided his clinical insights, especially via his sensitive and significant work within personal construct theory. Professor Vern Quinsey has helped me clarify my own views on sexual offenders probably more than he knows. Although Vern and I would agree now on few points surrounding the nature of sexual offending, Vern allowed me as a doctoral student the freedom to pursue my own course even when my direction veered from his own.

I am indebted to the many clients with whom I have worked over the years, especially those who have agreed to participate in various research projects. While all of our therapeutic encounters may not have been joyous occasions, I have taken lessons from all of them. I also want to thank the Augustana Faculty of the University of Alberta for providing me with sabbatical leave that facilitated the completion of this manuscript.

Finally, but far from least, my wife, Professor Jan Clarke, has helped me to formulate and to reformulate ideas by providing a patient ear and the insights of a feminist sociologist. I certainly could not have completed this work, or many of my previous studies, without Jan's assistance and support.

Chapter I

Sexual offending

An alternative construction

> The girl led me on ... she was teasing ... [although] I could be highly sexed.
>
> (E. S., incarcerated for the sexual assault of a young teenager, personal communication)

Sexual assault has become a major social issue in many contemporary cultures. It is rare to find any media broadcast that does not devote at least one story to the assault or abuse of someone, or to the concern about the potential consequences for assault victims. Considerable ink and airtime is devoted to stories about the backgrounds of various abusers and victims. The sexual abuse of individuals, especially those victims viewed as very vulnerable such as women and children, is rarely tolerated in any form in most societies. Perhaps part of the concern is due to some astonishing statistics concerning the incidence and prevalence of sexual assault in many countries. One national survey in the United States (Finkelhor *et al.*, 1990), for example, found that 25 per cent of adult female respondents and 16 per cent of adult male respondents reported some unwanted sexual touching or abuse. Published in 2002, national data from Canada (reported by Kong *et al.*, 2003) revealed a sexual assault rate of 86 per 100,000 residents. Whatever forms the basis of the concern about sexual assault and abuse, the concern is significant.

The discussions that swirl around sexual assault and abuse touch on many different issues, including morality, but legal issues involving sexual offenses that have psychological implications seem especially germane. There are a number of issues within criminal justice that are relevant to sexual offenses, and many of the issues and questions pertain to the offenders themselves. How are we to view these offenders, most often men, who perpetrate such unspeakable crimes? Often, especially since the mid-twentieth century, the answer has come back that, while they are generally not "psychotic" or "crazy", they do suffer from some form of mental defect or personality problem. The exact nature of the problem or problems of sexual abusers, however, is not at all clear.

In this book, some of the issues concerning sexual offenders, especially the nature of sexual assault and change in those who perpetrate such offenses, will be discussed. It is necessary to state at the outset some limits on this discussion. First, since much of the existing literature on sexual offenders deals with men as abusers, and all of my research and clinical experience have focussed on male offenders, I have decided to restrict the material in this book to men. In this way, my general use of "he", the gendered third-person personal pronoun, is justified. Female offenders may be very different from male offenders, but at this point we really do not know. More importantly, rather than a wide-ranging examination of a variety of different perspectives, a single theoretical framework will be presented. Personal construct theory (PCT), a psychological theory of human functioning that dates from the 1950s, appears to me to open up a number of possibilities in conceptualization, psychological assessment, and psychotherapeutic treatment of sexual offenders. This perspective has informed my research and clinical work with sexual offenders for more than two decades. The specific assessments and treatments that I have employed will be presented in some detail here. Although there will be very little discussion of more traditional approaches to work with sexual offenders, except to compare and contrast the personal construct approach, it is my hope that some of the specific techniques described here will be considered, if not employed by all forensic mental health professionals who work with sexual offenders. My real intent is that most if not all mainstream approaches to sexual offenders be re-examined in light of the alternative perspective, personal construct theory, presented in this book.

I would also note here that the quotations at the beginnings of the chapters are direct quotes provided by clients in writing that I have chosen to illustrate some point. These men, not identified in any specific way, do have important comments to make. I want to allow them an opportunity to share their own questions and comments about themselves in their own words. While they can be evasive, these men can also be insightful, not only into their own personal circumstances but into their fellows' conditions as well. If nothing else, they can illustrate well some point or issue at hand. All too often we ignore the voices of our clients, perhaps because we are too busy or, perhaps more likely, we see them as offering little to our "objective" assessment and treatment efforts except intentional diversion and obfuscation of the "truth". We should, however, take them seriously because they might well have something important to offer about the nature of deviant sexual interests or sexual abuse.

Before delving into the perplexing and troubling world of sexual offenses, an examination of human sexuality in more general terms is informative and provides a starting point. If nothing else, such a discussion can frame the more narrow concerns of deviant sexuality. In light of the extensive contemporary literature on human sexuality, only a brief overview of some relevant considerations on sexuality is possible to avoid complete distraction, and even another book.

Reflections on human sexuality

There is a significant difference between human and infrahuman sexual behaviour. On the whole, despite some well-publicized attempts to tie us to biological imperatives (e.g., Buss, 1994), theorists and therapists concerned with human sexuality are agreed on this basic statement. People are not bound to biophysical markers or instinctual demands as are most animals (Masters, *et al.*, 1988). Human sexual behaviours are not simply an immediate response to a particular colour, a smell, or a sound. Sex among humans is not simply a case of instinctive or automatic responses to various stimuli. We take a vast array of contextual features into consideration before responding in a sexual manner. It is not just the naked body of a desirable individual, however attractive, that elicits a sexual response from the human observer. Should the naked individual be pursued by a knife-wielding attacker, or sitting on a concrete floor of a grimy institution among other naked individuals, a sexual response is unlikely. The setting or the situation is key to human sexual behaviour, indeed all human behaviour. We tend to think, and interpret, before we act sexually. Understanding what kind of behaviour is called for by a situation is key to our adaptation and survival and, while we may question the quality of our thinking both individually and collectively on many occasions, it is certainly a key human characteristic.

An important determinant of human sexual response is mood. This is not in reference to the setting (e.g., "mood lighting", "mood music"), but mood here refers to the emotional-psychological state of the actor(s). It is important to be "in the mood" for sex, and this is not the case of monthly or annual sexual receptivity as is the case with many infrahumans. We are able to be sexual almost anytime, but we need to "feel" that it is the right time to engage in sexual behaviour. To be primed for sexual activity – to be "horny" or "randy" if you will – does not simply involve certain biophysical factors (e.g., healthy vascular system, presence of hormones in the bloodstream) although, no doubt, biophysical aspects of our bodies are important in such a state. More importantly, a sense of being ready for sex involves feelings of love, attraction to beauty, receptiveness to sensuality, excitement, and/or any number of other thoughts and emotions. Possibly a complex combination of feelings is necessary for any individual to become sexually aroused, or to be "in the mood", and we can also be put off sex rather readily at times simply by a transitory happening that breaks the mood. The necessary precursors in terms of feelings are probably very idiosyncratic, even if we can speak of common feelings that accompany sexual arousal (Masters *et al.*, 1988).

Interpretation is likely a key process in human sexual arousal and behaviour, and not just interpretation in terms of internal feelings or states, but interpretation of bodily states and sensations. Many if not all our bodily states require some understanding or "meaning" placed on the event (e.g., "Does that growling coming from my stomach mean I am hungry or did I pick up a nasty parasite in the tropics last month?"). If a man wakes in the morning with an erection and chooses to construe his stiff penis as evidence of sexual arousal rather than blood pooling in his lower abdomen as a function of a full bladder, there is every likelihood that the response will be sexual in nature rather than excretory. While there may be some frequent, common, or normative understandings of many bodily states, we still need to interpret bodily cues, often ambiguous ones but sometimes rather obvious ones, in order to act.

Just as the timing of human sexual expression is virtually limitless, almost anytime and anywhere, the range of sexual interests and behaviours engaged in by people is vast. Whether alone or with others, we engage in a wide range of activities that can be construed as sexual. Not all of these behaviours result in an orgiastic finale, although many might. Kinsey and colleagues (e.g., Kinsey *et al.*, 1948, 1953), despite methodological difficulties, did demonstrate in a series of detailed surveys in the mid-twentieth century that the heartland of the United States was not nearly as homogeneous, sexually speaking, as many believed it to be. The practices and fantasies of many Americans were much richer than even many so-called experts anticipated. This appears to be the case not only in the United States but around the world, across culture and time, even if many are not as ready to admit in face-to-face questioning the details that many of Kinsey's respondents offered. Sexual practice, indeed gender itself (see Weeks, 1995; Kinsman, 1996), is much more complex than many once believed. I would argue that explanations require a corresponding complexity. If we adopt a simple biological hedonism that seems at the basis of some views of human sexuality (e.g., Buss, 1994), how are we to explain variations? Theories have been developed, including a few longstanding and rather intriguing efforts (e.g., Freund, 1990), but most have proved to be too general, too vague, or too descriptive to be of much use. How can we account for the mind-numbing range and complexity of this sexual expression? This only appears possible if we consider the vast number of possibilities in terms of human sexual outcomes. In other words, people do not engage in sex for a single purpose. We do not engage in sex for reasons strictly of reproduction or physical pleasure; rather, as meaning-makers, we engage in sexual behaviour, and all behaviour, in response to a broad and varied set of possible meanings of the actions. The meanings of human sexual behaviour or the reasons for human sexual thoughts, feelings, and action are likely as varied and unique as there are individuals. For some individuals, sex may be only about reproduction and, for others, only pleasure, but sex can and probably does stand for much more for the majority of individuals. Sexual thoughts and behaviour can be for purposes of expressing love, expressing hate, expressing disgust, wanting to fall asleep, needing distraction from regularity, needing regularity, confirming attractiveness, advancing a relationship, achieving intimacy, and so on. A recent survey (Meston and Buss, 2007) found 237 distinct reasons for human sexual behaviour, including "Getting closer to God" and "Wanting to humiliate the person". I rather doubt, too, that students at the University of Texas, mostly undergraduates, are all that experienced or sophisticated in sexual realms. It is possible, if not probable, that a single sexual act can have multiple meanings and purposes. We need to consider not only personal attitudinal and emotional factors, but larger cultural and subcultural contexts (Masters *et al.*, 1988).

It also appears as if sexual expression and orientation are far more fluid than fixed throughout the course of life. Kinsman (1991, 1996) has argued that orientation, such as interest in same and opposite sex individuals, waxes and wanes over time for many individuals to the extent that they are reluctant to talk of dominant individual sexual orientations. They are certainly unwilling to ascribe significant genetic or biological roots to such notions as "homosexuality" or "heterosexuality".

If human sexual behaviour is so complex and multifaceted, is it possible to make any general statements about sex? At the risk of oversimplification, I would argue that we can. For me, human sexuality, being about personal meaning, revolves around self-validation and personal identity. By this, I do not mean that sex is necessarily selfish. Instead, sex, whether autoerotic behaviour or acts involving one or more partners, ultimately concerns an affirmation of the individual actor. This may be the affirmation, for example, of selflessness, insofar as someone views a particular sexual encounter as a demonstration of his or her own selfless giving. It is true that we may benefit collectively from sex, if only from the sustenance of further offspring, but the sexual act is essentially an individual one based on the views and the interests/desires/concerns of individual actors.

The adoption of a self-validational position can help to explain the vast varieties of human sexual interests and expressions. How, for example, can pain be pleasurable? How can being whipped or bound in a sadomasochistic encounter be a sensual delight? Unless one subscribes to some position that people can be "wired incorrectly", where painful stimuli like being slapped or whipped are actually perceived as pleasurable, the basic hedonistic assumptions of the position make anything "aberrant" very difficult to explain. If, however, we can adopt a more flexible agentic position whereby an individual is viewed as an active construer of his or her own world, pleasure and pain become very subjective and personal. Clearly, even a soft caress of the cheek is not in and of itself pleasant. It depends on the situation and the relationships between those involved. An unwanted touch, however gentle, can sting like a whip. If so, why cannot the reverse be true as well? The crack of the whip, or even the cut of the knife, might well be perceived by the recipient as the ultimate in sensual delights. Both context and construal are key factors. A cut on the cheek or leg from the razor is an event that draws blood and appears irritating and unpleasant regardless of the circumstances, probably with few exceptions. On the other hand, if the cut comes during a role-playing encounter staged by two individuals keen on mutual pleasure, either as part of a long-term sexual relationship or a brief affair lasting a few hours, the resulting sensation may well be much less irritating. In fact, especially in contrast to the cut during a morning shave, it may be very exciting and arousing. Thought about the nature of the situation and one's role in the action is important, as is one's overall view of oneself and any other players in the sexual encounter. Being tied up and punished by a stranger or an abuser may be extremely unpleasant, if not traumatic, whereas being punished by a lover or dominatrix may be arousing. This may, in part, be due to a view that the "pain" is justified because one is "bad", if only temporarily.

A long-term view of oneself as unworthy or unacceptable in some fashion may well provide a backdrop for the perception of continual pain and humiliation as quite acceptable if not pleasurable. It may also be that, as part of a generally overall positive view of oneself, the pain is perceived as pleasure if there is an understanding of oneself as "sexual adventurer". The pleasure, here, is the result of self-validation insofar as my view of myself as flawed, unworthy, domineering, liberated, or whatever is supported and extended by the "abuse" or sexual outcome. The resultant self-knowledge or affirmation of current self-understanding is inherently pleasant or satisfying. This position requires further elaboration and exploration, and I will soon situate it in a well-developed theory of personality.

Popular perspectives on deviant sexual behaviour

The basis of much contemporary thought on sexual offenders and sexual deviance dates from the nineteenth century. A number of psychiatric investigators, especially the German psychiatrist Krafft-Ebing (1886/1960), in an attempt to understand and categorize the variety of what must have appeared to Victorian eyes as a bewildering range of bizarre and troubling practices, developed theories and hypotheses about the nature of normal and abnormal sexual practices. A number of historians and sociologists (e.g., Foucault, 1976/1990; Lutzen, 1995; Weeks, 1995) have described the historical origins of this medico-scientific position, as well as the medicalization of sexuality. In the realm of perversity, Krafft-Ebing was one of the first to attempt a psychiatric nosology of abnormal sexual practices and behaviour. Krafft-Ebing (1886/1965), in his famous text on deviant sexual practices that went into many editions, *Psychopathia sexualis*, documented eventually hundreds of cases of non-normative human sexual practice on his way to developing a systematic categorization. He coined many of the terms still in use in psychiatry today (e.g., pedophilia, exhibitionism), and his efforts formed the basis of psychiatric thought on contemporary sexual deviation. According to

Foucault (1976/1990), the mid- to late nineteenth century marked the beginning of what he termed "sexual science". The intent, no doubt, of the work by Krafft-Ebing and others was to shift a class of behaviour that was both curious and disturbing from moral and religious domains to medical areas. Such a move would render them open to scientific solution or treatment. As expected, the treatment focus did indeed shift from religious interventions (e.g., confession) to somatic therapies and, eventually, psychotherapies. For Foucault, however, this represented the pathologizing of all non-normative sexual practices, especially homosexuality.

From the early to mid-twentieth century, with a few noteworthy exceptions (e.g., Ellis, 1933), academic interest in deviant sexual behaviour seemed to stagnate. Even Sigmund Freud, despite an early interest in the importance of child sexual abuse in the development of adult psychopathology and the psychosexual theory that is so well-known today, had remarkably little to say about sexual perversion. As Masson (1984) described in detail, Freud's abandonment of his tentative seduction hypothesis of the late 1890s led him away from concern about actual sexual abuse to sexual fantasy. Freud (1905/1975) did note later, however, that "the sexual abuse of children is found with uncanny frequency among school teachers and child attendants" (p. 14). He concluded, rather weakly, that "the impulses of sexual life are among those which, even normally, are the least controlled by the higher activities of the mind" (p. 15). One subsequent psychoananalytic writer (Fraser, 1976) has provided an account of child sexual abuse from a Freudian perspective. In a very creative and well-crafted book, Fraser has described child molesters as the result of a dominant yet distant mother and an absent, weak or "despised" father. The unresolved Oedipal strivings of a young male in such a family produces a "narcissistic inversion" in which the individual, as he ages, "remains deeply in love with the child he was then" (p. 20). He concluded, perhaps correctly, that the major problem faced by men who molest children is their obsessive preoccupation with their sexually deviant behaviour. Fraser draws widely from English literature to support his case. His theory, unfortunately, is unconvincing. Not only does Fraser relate homosexuality to child sexual abuse – to be fair, a problem with psychoanalysis generally as well as other contemporary thought – but he fails to account adequately for adult males who molest young females since they are the wrong sex to be "the child he was then". His argument is weakened, undoubtedly, by his failure to consult the clinical and/or research literatures seriously. An intensive examination of one child molester was conducted by Bell and Hall (1971) from a psychodynamic if not psychoanalytic perspective. Their case study of an abuser focussed on dream content and dream analysis. Their position was that latent dream symbols are used to represent significant but disturbing thoughts and feelings. Among their findings, these investigators reported that their molester, a single adult male who lived with his mother, had numerous dreams that involved his mother, supportive of the psychoanalytic view that dominant mothers, or at least the perception of a dominant mother, are a causative factor for many if not all abusers.

One popular psychological theory employed at times to explain sexual abuse is social learning theory (e.g., Abel *et al.*, 1984). From a social learning perspective, a number of theorists (e.g., Abel *et al.*, 1984; Laws and Marshall, 1990) have argued that children can be exposed to models and experience some early arousal to non-normal stimuli which, when combined with inappropriate masturbatory fantasies during the adolescent years, lead to sexually anomolous behaviour. At the same time, in line with more recent work in social learning theory (e.g., Bandura, 1982, 1986), cognitions in the form of "self-descriptions which may guide or limit ... behavior" (Laws and Marshall, 1990, p. 220) are recognized as significant in the acquisition and maintenance of sexually deviant behaviours. There has, however, been relatively little explicit use of social learning theory over the past several years. This is surprising given the concern of cognitive social learning theory (Bandura, 1986) on the regulation of behaviour.

A portion of the empirical work on sexual offenders' cognitions has been concerned with fantasy, especially deviant sexual fantasy, and to a somewhat lesser extent on deviant beliefs and attributions. A fairly direct line can be traced back to a New Jersey study of 300 sexual offenders by Ellis and Brancale (1956). This early work was not concerned with offenders' cognition – quite surprising given Ellis's (e.g., Ellis, 1962) developing interest in irrational beliefs – except in terms of offenders' accounts of their own offenses. Among their results, they cited non-specific "clinical evidence" that exhibitionists and child molesters tend to have difficulty explaining their own motives. They failed, however, to make differential predictions for offender types, with most of their discussion assuming that sexual offenders represented a homogeneous group.

If this were a more traditional overview of sexual offending and sexual deviation, we would likely have to include a serious discussion of the paraphilias. The paraphilias, or literally "disorders of brotherly love", provide the classificatory label for deviant or abnormal sexual behaviours developed by the American Psychiatric Association (APA, 1980, 2000). There are, however, a number of problems with this notion. The first and most obvious difficulty with the paraphilias concerns the term itself. Since we are concerned here with sexual behaviour, where is the relevance of "brotherly love"? Also, even if we adopted the more appropriate "paraeros", the entire issue of misplaced love, as opposed to simply abusive sexual behaviour, would remain. Since I actually see paraeros as doing a severe disservice to the term eros or erotica, I am not suggesting seriously replacing existing terminology. It, and all related terms, should be eliminated completely rather than modified.

Another problem with the paraphilias concerns the limitation of the category. As noted by Marshall (2006) and other writers, the exclusion of those who engage in sexually coercive behaviour with adults, typically called "rapists", is problematic. This exclusion no doubt reveals significant social assumptions and values of the largely male *Diagnostic and Statistical Manual* (DSM) organizing committee of the American Psychiatric Association, and probably makes an important statement about how "normal" rape is perceived by a broader public audience.

A further problem with this approach concerns the legal and conceptual jumble of disorders in the current version of the *DSM*. Some of the sexual disorders considered paraphilias, such as transvestism or masochism, do not refer to criminal acts in many jurisdictions. Hence, they are strange bedfellows with such notions as pedophilia, or sexual involvement with children, that tend to refer to criminal behaviour. Again, even if these issues were addressed, another significant obstacle would remain.

The paraphilias, as a psychiatric nosological category, are commonly accepted to have a biological or biochemical basis (e.g., Bradford, 1990; Langevin, 1990). Even careful investigators like Hucker and Bain (1990), who recognize the contributions of social processes and thought concerning social experience, would point to the importance of biochemicals like serum testosterone in male offenders. The specific nature of the problem is often viewed simply as an excess of serum testosterone in male offenders, and not only in those who are sexually aggressive with adults but all sex offenders (Bradford, 1990). Overall, the paraphilias are accepted by psychiatrists and medically oriented clinical psychologists as having a biogenic albeit largely unknown origin. The power of the medico-scientific position is undeniable. It stands not just as a beacon, calling the faithful and/or warning those who stray, but imposes itself on the constructions of those who might see an alternative. For a number of reasons, I would argue that we need an alternative that is more meaningful and avoids existing problems created by such a broad categorization.

The psychiatric nosology that is the DSM seems to be a creature that has turned on its creator, pathologizing everything and everyone in its path. It has grown from a relatively limited manual in the 1950s and 1960s (APA, 1952, 1968) to a monstrocity by the turn of the twenty-first century (APA, 2000). Practically all behaviour that strays from the acceptable, tranquil norms of middle-of-the-road Western life is deemed a clinical syndrome or due to some type of psychopathology (Raskin and Epting, 1993; Caplan, 1995). The unfortunate direction that this self-sustaining approach has taken is one and the same as the international pharmaceutical industry because increased pathology leads to increased medication use. This is unfortunate because, setting aside larger issues of the overmedication of many individuals and the necessity of many medications, it dictates a symptom management approach. The roots of the problem become secondary to addressing and controlling the expressions of the disorder. When it comes to sex offender treatment, a common first attempt is for a forensic psychiatrist to prescribe anti-androgen medication. This treatment, designed to reduce testosterone levels in the bloodstream and body of a male offender, may well control deviant behaviour in some men for some time (see Bradford, 1990), but the long-term efficacy of the treatment is very moot at this point.

Another more significant concern for me involves the psychological impact of the psychodiagnostic process (see Raskin and Epting, 1993; Honos-Webb and Leitner, 2001). Many sexual offenders seem legitimately baffled, at least when young or when first aware of their interests or involvements. Their confusion makes them keen for any explanation of their sexual behaviour. Once an official diagnosis is offered, however provisional, there is a tendency to regard it as "real" or "fact", and the diagnosis takes on a life of its own. Many offenders, while perhaps relieved initially that they now "know" what produced their puzzling and revolting lapse in judgement, soon find them-selves looking to confirm the diagnosis in various ways. At the very least, this can produce negative affect, such as depression and anxiety. They can also experience negative affect if presented with various and competing diagnoses, which is not at all uncommon. What is most serious from my perspective is that the process of self-fulfilling prophecy can produce a committment to the diagnosis and increase the likelihood of reoffense. More on the process of self-labelling in the next chapter, but suffice it to state here that the effects of labelling appear real and serious.

One final point about the process of psychodiagnosis and sexual offending: all categorization necessarily involves a loss of information as individuals are forced into categories for the sake of parsimony. As is commonly stated in the psychiatric clinic, pure types are rare (Silverman, 1983). Even if an individual appears to be an exemplar of a particular diagnosis, some important infor-mation may be overlooked following the diagnosis. Most mental health professionals, especially those rushed and overworked by crushing caseloads, see diagnoses rather than people, much less highly unique individuals. Any information lost or not recorded because it is seen as irrelevant for a diagnosis is possibly key to a successful intervention. The use of psychodiagnoses, really just Procrustean beds, therefore, should be avoided if for no other reason than concerns about treatment efficacy.

Personal construct theory, linked to an assessment strategy and set of psychotherapeutic interventions, appears to a number of us who work with offenders as helpful in forensic settings (see Horley, 1988a, 2003b; Needs, 1988; Houston, 1998). Interventions with sexual offenders, in particular, are high on my list of applications of this theory (Horley, 2003a). Among other advantages, this integrated and systematic theory avoids all need to engage in either–or categorization of clients.

Personal construct theory and abnormal behaviour

In 1955, George Kelly, a clinical psychologist from the United States, pub-lished two volumes presenting in detail a theory of personality that he called personal construct theory (PCT). Kelly offered a theory of personality deeply rooted in clinical practice, but he also described a philosophical perspective at odds with the prevailing intellectual climate in psychology, as well as a methodology that attempted to blend idiographic or individual richness with statistical rigour. Over the five decades since the publication of this work, PCT has grown into a relatively influential perspective in psychology. Should any reader wish to pursue this literature in more depth, various reviews are helpful. Bonarius (1965) wrote the first major review of PCT research. Other reviews, including a major one focussing on methodology (Bannister and Mair,1968), an edited volume stressing theoretical and philosophical issues (Bannister, 1970), and one showing the relevance of PCT to different areas of psychology (Bannister and Fransella, 1971), appeared within a few years of Bonarius' effort. More recently, a monograph by Warren (1998) examined in more detail the philosophical connections and implications of PCT. A number of books written by and for clinicians have been published over the years. Epting (1984) and Landfield (Landfield and Epting, 1987; Landfield, 1970) are two notable contributors. Perhaps the most comprehensive review of clinical research and applications of PCT was provided by Winter (1992a).

Unlike most personality theorists, Kelly (1955, 1958b, 1963, 1969, 1970a) explicitly formulated the epistemological assumptions underlying his approach. His principle of constructive alternativism asserts that "reality" – and, according to Kelly, there is indeed a real world that we all must learn to deal with – does not reveal itself to us directly; rather, it is subject to as many alternative ways of interpreting it as we ourselves can invent. In this way, we can explain the rich diversity of human experience. Moreover, according to Kelly, all of our current representations of events are anticipatory in function. In order to predict our future experience, each individual develops a unique personal construct system and attempts to accommodate it to the unknown, or at least not completely known structure of reality. This system of constructs, including complex subsystems, is ordered hierarchically insofar as some constructs, superordinate ones, subsume other constructs, subordinate ones. In other words, use of "good", as one pole of a superordinate construct, implies that the event so-called is also "positive", "constructive", etc. (i.e., whatever the poles of subsumed constructs are). A construct system affords the underlying ground of coherence and unity in the ongoing experience of each person; in fact, our system is the sum total of each of us psychologically speaking.

Although any particular sequence of events lends itself to a variety of different interpretations, some ways of construing probably will prove more useful for anticipating similar events in the future. As events do not directly reveal their meanings to us, it must be the anticipatory constructions or hypotheses which we impose on them that endow them with whatever significance they may have in relation to our own behaviour. Thus, Kelly's constructive alternativism carries specific implications in terms of how human behaviour relates to both internal and external "stimulus" input. He explicitly argued that "one does not learn certain things from the nature of stimuli which play upon him, but only what his cognitive framework permits him to see in the stimuli" (Kelly, 1955, p. 75). For Kelly, people have the capacity to represent and to anticipate events, not merely respond to them, and each individual is personally responsible for choosing the specific constructions of events that will inform his or her actions.

In developing this model, Kelly avoided explicitly any distinction between scientists and the subjects of their inquiries. He asserted that all persons are scientists. As scientists, we attempt to describe, to explain, to predict, and to control events; in other words, we all seek to understand experience and to anticipate the future, whether a professionally trained scientist or not. In this way, Kelly applied a constructivist model of scientific activity to the explanation of all human behaviour. We need to acknowledge the reflexive nature of this theory because Kelly attempted to explain his own behaviour and not just his clients' actions. Each individual not only constructs his or her own hypotheses for anticipating events, but also evaluates and possibly revises them in the light of the results of behavioural experiments based on these hypotheses. Kelly (1970b) viewed all behaviour as experimental, with our personal experiments providing validation, or not, for current constructs and, thus, serving as the basis of future construction.

In terms of the implications of constructive alternativism, several authors have dealt specifically with the epistemology of the philosophical position. In an early analysis, Mischel (1964) analyzed Kelly's position in terms of the distinction between rule-following and causal explanations of behaviour, showing how PCT entailed a rule-following explanatory system. Mischel also addressed its implications for psychodiagnosis. Major contributions to the philosophical foundations of PCT appeared in Bannister's (1970) edited book. Here, the theory was examined as a perspective bearing close resemblance to several formulations including those by Wittgenstein (Shotter, 1970), existentialism (Holland, 1970), and common language philosophers (Leman, 1970). Little (1972) compared and contrasted the philosophical assumptions of PCT with those of psychoanalysis and behaviourism. He suggested that the model of the person-as-scientist is unnecessarily restrictive as a guide to inquiry within the field of personality, a point with which Yorke (1989) would agree, but for different reasons.

One clear strength of PCT is its central concern with choice and personal agency (see Chapter 2 for a more detailed discussion). People are active construers of their own experience, and they have the ability to choose for themselves construct pairs, their own placement within the construct, and specific behavioural experiments. This invokes the notions of will and willpower, lost and forgotten within much of twentieth-century psychology. A Kellian view of willpower, however, is not a view based on willpower as "thing", such as a personality trait (Fitch and Ravlin, 2005), but as "process". What we are able to do, we are able to undo; what we are able to construe, we are able to reconstrue.

There has been a decided emphasis in PCT on abnormal and clinical topics, especially empirical versus theoretical contributions. This is hardly surprising given Kelly's involvement in the establishment of clinical psychology in the United States (see Neimeyer, 1985, for a brief history). The contributions of PCT to abnormal and clinical psychology are noteworthy and require some examination here (but see Chapter 5 for more details). First, however, it seems necessary to describe briefly the PCT perspective on psychological assessment, even though a more detailed discussion will be presented later (see Chapter 4).

Kelly (1955) championed what he called a "credulous approach" to psychological assessment and treatment. If we as psychologists want to know what is happening with a client, we should ask him or her directly. This is not to ignore the importance of therapeutic interpretation in terms of making sense of what we are told, and it certainly does not suggest that every statement from a client be taken at face value. A direct method of questioning, however, is of utmost importance according to Kelly. A client's perspective must be requested and respected, avoiding the overinterpretation and hubris that comes from a doctor-knows-best position that appears implicit, if not explicit, in many psychotherapeutic camps. More will be said about this approach later, along with some of its implications, but the credulous approach was very much out of step with mid-twentieth-century behaviourism and psychoanalysis, dominant perspectives in psychology at the time Kelly's writings first appeared.

As is the case with his entire theory, Kelly's view of psychological and personality assessment is at odds with mainstream perspectives. The field of personality assessment, for example, tends to be divided among objective techniques, such as the Minnesota Multiphasic Personality Inventory (MMPI), and projective techniques, such as the Rorschach Inkblot Test. Kelly (1958a), however, viewed both types of tests with a jaundiced eye. His preferred approach was, appropriately, neither objective nor projective. He developed a number of different assessments (see Chapter 4), most notably the repertory grid technique, or rep grid. This matrix-based technique – really a methodology rather than a specific, standardized technique – allows an assessor to examine a very limited number of an assessee's personal constructs. While procedures and formats differ, the common format of rep grid elicits construct pairs and asks the assessee to compare and contrast various role elements, such as oneself and other individuals.

Bannister (1965) argued forcefully for the use of the rep grid, when working within the theoretical framework of PCT, in the study of abnormal behaviour because of its focus on the client's view of the world in his or her own terms. The rep grid was adapted to the specific problems of thought disorder by Bannister and Fransella (1966) in order to produce a clinically economic and adequately standardized grid test for detecting the presence of thought disorder in individuals often diagnosed as "schizophrenic". The Grid Test of Thought Disorder assumes, among other points, that many individuals clinically designated as "schizophrenic" manifest very weak and unstable relationships between their constructs (Bannister *et al.*, 1971). This work is rooted deeply in PCT. Kelly suggested that a highly complex set of constructs, typical of individuals called "schizoid", fails to function as a whole because the constructs lack sufficient ranges of convenience to enable the person to relate one construct to another (see Bannister and Mair, 1968). Early research by Bannister and colleagues (e.g., Bannister *et al.*, 1975) did reveal differences between those labelled "schizophrenic" and so-called "normals", although the exact nature of the differences, or their interpretation, was far from accepted (see McPherson and Buckley, 1970; Bannister, 1972, 1973; Frith and Lillie, 1972; Haynes and Phillip, 1973; McPherson *et al.*, 1973; Radley, 1974). These early investigations, along with the original views on psychopathology from Kelly (1955), led to a important focus within PCT concerning problems with construct structure. There has also been some research into psychological problems based on construct content, although to a lesser extent (Winter, 1992a). Before discussing these overarching issues in more detail, a brief discussion of the general nature of personal constructs and construct systems appears necessary.

According to Kelly (1955), all human experience is interpreted. There is no "brute reality" impinging on us and our psychological processes; rather we attempt to make sense of all of the daily events that comprise our lives on this earth. This is not to say that there is no "real world" – there is a concrete reality that exists beyond each individual – but we as humans do not know it directly. We can only interpret and attempt to make sense of our personal experience. The means by which we break our flow of experience into meaningful "chunks" is via abstraction and the use of our own somewhat unique and somewhat common constructs. Our personal constructs are bipolar, or binary if you will, lenses through which the world is considered. "Up–down", "male–female", "night–day", "good–bad", "tall–short", and "black–white" are but a few of the examples of construct pairs employed by people. The poles of a construct pair are not necessarily diametric opposites, although some problems with interpretation arise as construct poles become increasingly orthogonal or unrelated, and Kelly (1955) argued that direct opposition in construct poles provides optimal construal. This is not to suggest that we necessarily or should view the world in strict, "black versus white" terms. Indeed, as we age, we likely do come to view events in more complex ways, when "black–white" is differentiated into "black–not black" and "white–not white", permitting us to recognize shades of grey if not many colours.

We necessarily employ many thousands or tens of thousands of different constructs in order to construe and to reconstrue our experience, whether the interactions we have with people and objects or the internal biophysical world of our individual bodies. Kelly (1955) and later PCT theorists are not specific in terms of how many constructs we employ typically. Regardless of numbers of constructs, we need to make sense of experience in order to discern patterns or to formulate hypotheses, as any good scientist would, about the nature of things and coming events. Like scientists, we are constantly attempting to describe, to explain, to predict, and to control our life experiences. Although Kelly (1955) himself argued that we tend to be tantalized by the future rather than concerned with the past, hence his emphasis on prediction and control rather than "mere" description and explanation, I think there is a case to be made for more human variation in terms of temporal orientation, and I would argue that, for some of us, perhaps the chroniclers or storytellers, the past is more of a focus of construal as we attempt to describe and to explain, perhaps with a partial aim of informing ourselves and others about important experiential patterns.

However many or few personal constructs we may possess, they are not all equal in terms of importance, or at least level of use. Our constructs are arranged, according to Kelly (1955), in a complex hierarchy. Some construct pairs exist at a higher ordinal level with respect to others. A more superordinate construct pair, such as "good–bad", might be used to understand people, but by employing such a construct pair I might also be viewing a "good person" as "honest", "hard-working", and "God-fearing". In other words, all subordinate constructs are implied or taken for granted when a superordinate construct is applied. Our construct system too is composed of various subsystems, or arrangements of hierarchically ordered constructs that may or may not have any relationship to each other. A lack of relationship, for Kelly (1955), is not a problem; indeed, a certain degree of psychological fragmentation is likely in any healthy person. From a PCT perspective, we are not so aware or concerned with cognitive consistency on a daily basis as many psychologists would argue, and this allows us to go about affairs that may involve a certain degree of psychological incompatibility (e.g., a devoutly committed Christian who is also a committed biologist).

Our personal constructs, in a sense, form the building blocks of human consciousness. They permit us to interpret life experience and to figure out what might befall us should we attempt any particular course of action. Construing a brick wall as "hard" as opposed to "soft" can allow an individual to avoid a broken nose, or worse, by restricting attempts to walk into or through such entities. They are behind all of the behavioural experiments that we may choose to perform at any time. Should an experiment fail, a construct pair might be discarded entirely, or it may simply be used with a different set of elements, other people or perhaps employed simply with non-human objects. In this way, constructs come and go, yet most of us probably retain a set of relatively consistent constructs because we have found that, over time, they have proved their worth in our personal experiments and we need them, perhaps regularly or just on a rare occasion, in order to understand events. PCT, therefore, is a theory about psychological stability and change – it allows us to explain both personal consistency and inconsistency. Our constructs and construct system are constantly undergoing revision, modulation, based on various experiential cycles presented and discussed by Kelly (1955). Such a discussion would take us too far afield at this time, but suffice it to say that PCT takes a very dynamic stance with respect to psychological processing. We are active and constant construers of our life experiences.

A couple of qualifications about the nature of personal constructs seem required. First, PCT is not simply a theory about psycholinguistics. All constructs do not involve labels or linguistic referents. All of us likely employ some constructs, and perhaps many for some of us that defy verbal labels. They are more like "intuitions", "feelings", or "just a sense", yet they still permit us to make sense of events, or the people and things that comprise the events in our everyday lives. While one person might describe an undesirable individual as "creepy" or "obnoxious", a second person might avoid the same individual but describe the avoidant behaviour as due to "a vibe" or "a feeling that I can't describe in words". In short, not all of our experiences that make sense need to be translated into words, although this might be our most common means of constructing our constructions. Second, and related to the previous point, PCT is not simply a theory about cold, rational thought. Kelly (1955) was loath to distinguish between "affect" and "cognition", a very traditional distinction within psychology, because he did not want to create a false distinction. He certainly did not want his theory known as a cognitive theory, yet he no doubt anticipated correctly that this is how it would be viewed, and indeed it has. Affect within PCT is bound inextricably with construal processes. Although the exact nature of affect has not been developed in detail within PCT, both Kelly (1955) and McCoy (1977, 1981) have described it as a companion to or a consequence of construal processes. Specific affective experiences have been described by each writer. Kelly (1955), for example, described guilt as a result of dislodgement from core role constructs, or an experience that is the result of acting counter to how a person perceives himself or herself centrally (e.g., behaving cruelly while construing oneself as kind), while McCoy (1977) defined happiness as the awareness of the validation of some core constructs.

The stage now appears set for a brief discussion of the nature of psychological problems within PCT. How does construction become dysfunctional? One major distinction here concerns structural versus content-related problems (see Winter, 1992a). Structure refers to the nature of constructs with respect to elements, as well as the relations between constructs and construct subsystems. First, let us consider construct–element relations.

All of our personal constructs can be applied only to a limited range of events, people, or things, or elements to use the terminology of PCT. Some constructs, for example "good", might be used to interpret many elements, including people and things, but they will not be able to be applied to every possible element. We might speak sensibly about "good friends" and "good trees", yet have difficulty describing "good prime numbers". For some of us, goodness as a construct may have very narrow applicability – we might, for example, only apply the term "good" to certain individuals who believe in a very narrow set of beliefs (like us?), whereas trees can best be seen as "useful" or not. Sometimes, or for some of us very frequently, we are able to employ constructs to make sense of a very limited range of elements, with no others ever allowed near such constructs. While such impermeable constructs might be adaptive in some circumstances, they might lead to a very rigid and narrow frame of reference. On the other hand, if we have a large number of constructs that include a very wide range of elements, we might be able to construe efficiently but perhaps only simply with a limited number of constructs. To a great extent, a PCT perspective does not make categorical judgements about structural aspects of construing because it does depend on the specific conditions that an individual is dealing with as to the suitability of their style and type of construal patterns. Even a preemptive thinker, a person who only tends to see people as "good or bad" and events as "this way or that way", we might condemn generally as simplistic, but there are many situations where this can be a highly adaptive psychological frame. In times of war, during certain business meetings, and during conflict situations in a maximum-secure prison (which I have witnessed first-hand all too often), there can be no tolerance for the shades of grey or moral relativism that might result from more complex constructions such as "good–not good" and "bad–not bad", the result of splitting a construct pair "good–bad". He or she who hesitates can be lost, and simplistic consideration of alternatives might facilitate quick and successful decisions. It really depends on the many factors – environmental, interpersonal, and intrapersonal – that impinge on us during any event.

When it comes to the assignment of an element to a construct pole, often for many of us there is little variation. A person is "tall" rather than "short", and that is the end of that. At times, and for some of us more than others, however, there can be considerable vacillation. Elements can shift quite easily from one construct pole to the other. Consideration of events from diametrically opposed positions can be a fruitful exercise. For Kelly (1955), this is a matter of loose construing, and it is neither pathological nor non-pathological in and of itself. Loose construing likely aids in creativity, although perhaps only in the presence of a degree of tightening, but it can be at the basis of serious confusion and, over the long run, probably at the basis of thought disorder. Tightness alone is likely maladaptive unless someone lived in an unchanging world, and it has been implicated in a variety of psychological difficulties, such as depression (see Space and Cromwell, 1980). An ability to both loosen and tighten our interpretations and understandings of events probably separates the genius from the mad person.

As Winter (1992a) noted, there has been relatively little research into construct content compared to construct structure. There are, however, good reasons to examine the specific constructs that an individual employs. Some work (e.g., Horley, 1988a; Horley and Quinsey, 1995) has been done with sexual offenders' constructs, and this will be discussed later. In a general sense, it may be important to see what types of constructs are employed by certain individuals, or groups of individuals. According to Kelly (1955), optimal construing involves construct poles that tend towards orthogonal relations rather than oblique relations. In other words, logical opposition is better to sort elements on a construct pair versus something less than complete opposition. When construct pairs display less than a 180-degree relationship, they are described as "bent". On occasion, when an individual's construct pair shows no apparent connection whatsoever, it is necessary to question the person to find out the particular meaning of terms because the construct terminology may be very idiosyncratic and may mean something very different to the assessee than assessor. Sometimes, however, given no distinct meaning, and given no mistaken attempt to combine two different construct pairs, some construct pairs are just very oblique. In my work with extremely thought disordered individuals in psychiatric hospitals, very bent constructs can be revealed. One 20-year-old inpatient that I remember quite clearly, a pleasant yet vacant young man who looked about constantly with large and unblinking eyes, provided a construct pair of "nice vs. person". After questioning him about this and some similar construct pairs, thinking that he failed to understand the nature of the assessment task that I was asking him to complete, he declared that he understood completely, and this was how he thought about the elements that were presented. Later, I wondered if he was telling me that all people were not very nice from his perspective, or whether this contrast was simply a random selection of a pair of commonly associated words, as in "She's a nice person." Whatever the case, he and other clients have shown me what I would regard as very odd construct pairs, or at least ones that would provide much difficulty in making any reasonable interpretations of other people and things. Such construct pairs may reflect the thought disorder as well as contribute to it. Other aspects of construct content related to psychological problems, such as the use or avoidance of constructs related to emotion, have been linked to various problems (see Winter, 1992a, for a summary).

Rather than report in detail on the range of empirical literature that has been generated over the past half century within abnormal and clinical psychology, it might be better to get on with the specific concern of the present book, a discussion of sexual offending. There is one point, however, that I would make of a general nature before leaving the PCT view and research on psychological problems. Over the past decade or two, there is a noticeable drift within the PCT camp toward research on "disorders" such as psychopathy, schizophrenia, and posttraumatic stress disorder. I regard this as a regrettable development, and one that is out of step with Kelly's original direction for PCT. I do not believe that we can question the nature of such disorders yet reify them and treat them as real and significant. This trend in PCT research and clinical work likely speaks to the power of the dominant medical model in psychology and psychiatry, but it is not how personal construct theorists and therapists should proceed. However clumsy it may be, this book will only refer to psychiatric diagnoses in quotations or some such similar manner.

One area within abnormal and clinical psychology addressed by PCT in the past decade or so is the assessment and treatment of criminal offenders (Needs, 1988; Horley, 2003b). Criminal offending and other forensic psychological work has been addressed on occasion by early contributors to PCT (see Fransella and Adams, 1966; Landfield, 1971) but not in any systematic manner. The investigations done to date are very preliminary, in part because of the difficulty inherent in any alternative approach to the dominant framework, but they have provided an intriguing glimpse into criminal behaviour generally and sexual offending in particular. One of the broad implications for the field of sexual offending demands discussions here.

A dimensional view of deviant sexuality

PCT provides a very different perspective on deviant sexual behaviour from most theories. Offenders who victimize other individuals sexually are not viewed as offending against others due to a disease entity or some underlying disorder. Sexual offenders, like everyone whether behaving in an exploitative or abusive manner or not, act on a particular pattern and style of interpreting themselves and their fellows. In a general sense, rather than understand sexual perversion as a set of discrete categories, psychiatric or otherwise, we might better view sexual offenders dimensionally, or along a set of bipolar dimensions. An overarching view of sexual offenders might include a set of primary dimensions along which offenders – indeed, non-offenders too – could be placed and considered in relation to each other. A dimensional view would help to avoid any "hardening of the categories" (Kelly, 1969, p. 294), or a narrowness of focus that only allows us to refine and to alter our existing and perhaps defective constructions. I have no doubt that it would improve our therapeutic efforts with respect to sexual offenders. I will expand on this concern in subsequent chapters (see Chapter 5 in particular).

It is important at this point to make clear what a PCT-based dimensional view of deviant sexual behaviour would not include. Eysenck (1964, 1977) presented what he called a dimensional approach to personality and criminal behaviour. According to Eysenck (1964), there are two basic personality types or dimensions, extraversion–introversion and neuroticism–emotional stability. These two bipolar dimensions are biologically based, presumably present from birth, although Eysenck offered no evidence for his premises. Criminals, including sexual offenders, are individuals high in both extraversion and neuroticism. Later, Eysenck (1977) added high psychoticism to his understanding of the personality dimensions of criminals. Such a view, while perhaps dimensional, is a static dimensional view that rather simplistically groups all offenders in the same camp. Eysenck's approach is based very much on the personality trait, a very static and deterministic view of human psychology. Rather oddly, Eysenck prefaced the presentation of his theory with a discussion of the "Mark of Cain" in biblical scripture, where he argued that the Mark of Cain is evidence that the notion of a "born criminal" is well established in antiquity. While I would interpret the biblical tale as referring more to the right of the divine to mete out severe punishment for murder, making this a biblical injunction against capital punishment, such a discussion seems too far afield unless biblical support for a position is a requirement. The dimensional nature of PCT is not Eysenckian dimensionality because it is based on a unit of analysis much more dynamic than the personality type/trait, a very non-biblical notion I could add. Indeed, from a PCT perspective, we can interpret the three Eysenckian dimensions as professional constructs, rather preemptive and narrow ones at that, used to sort all individuals, offenders and non-offenders, into neat categories. All PCT dimensions are open to change and modification, if not total replacement. Therefore, any dimensions proposed here are temporary or transitory constructs necessarily.

While the dimensions that we choose to construe sex offenders might well vary over time, I would suggest two meaningful variables, activity and age, to begin consideration of sexual offenders. Activity refers to the nature of sexual activity, whether coercive or not. On the extreme of coercion, extreme physical force and physical damage, perhaps resulting in death of a victim, could be an anchor for such a scale. Threat, verbal or physical, or even minor physicality such as a push, might be a mid-point of activity. Non-coercive, consenting, and mutually pleasurable sexual activity might anchor the other pole of such a dimension. In this case, the actual sexual involvement is a concern rather than a slippery notion such as intention or preference.

Age may seem straightforward, but it is a difficult and perhaps controversial suggestion. Most observers might agree that prepubescent children are inappropriate sexual partners – hence, age from 0 to 14 years might be on one side of this dimension – but age-appropriate sexual partners are not necessarily easily defined. Some parties (e.g., APA, 2000) would see the elderly as inappropriate insofar as gerontophilia, a sexual attraction to older adults, is listed as a paraphilia in *DSM-IV-TR*. While this appears to me to smack of ageism, there could be arguments about the appropriateness of a wide age gap between sexual partners in the context of power relations and personal suitability. At the risk of inviting dispute, which no doubt would result regardless of the specific terminology, anchors, or metric suggested for such a variable, age might be included as a second dimension.

The resulting two-dimensional graph (see Figure 1.1) would allow users to place either individuals or groups in spatial relationships. Some metric or means by which to order the placement of chosen individuals or groups would have to be selected, but this is not a major difficulty, and multiple metrics could be used depending on one's specific concerns. One objection could be raised from a strict PCT perspective in terms of the bipolar nature of constructs: Do we not construe the world in terms of selection of one construct pole or the other? In this case, not unlike a two-dimensional analysis of a rep grid, we are superimposing a continuum on dimensional space but keeping in mind that activity and age, or whatever dimensions are selected, are simply summaries of many other underlying constructs. Dimensionality penetrates the graph at both a micro-level and a macro-level of analysis so, whatever our chosen graph appears like, it is only a small section of possible dimensional space.

Plotting individuals on a two-dimensional graph such as Figure 1.1 might also address a number of heuristic and research purposes. Placing offenders on meaningful axes relative to each other might facilitate grouping for a further particular assessment, or it might help select a therapy group using some form of cluster analysis. Should therapy be a primary concern, such a graph can provide a clear and tangible outcome (i.e., movement from the present quadrant into an adjacent one). It is also possible using a multi-dimensional graph to display multiple behaviours of a single individual. We might, for example, examine the last ten assaults of an individual offender to try to uncover connections between them, or perhaps simply the variation of a single person's deviant sexual acts for assessment and/or therapeutic purposes. The possible applications of this approach may be limitless.

Dimensionality might not encourage concise communication between mental health professions. Concise communication is presented as a strength of current psychiatric nosologies and the terminology employed by clinicians using such a system (APA, 2000). Given disputes over the real meaning of certain terms such as pedophilia (see Marshall, 2006), however, the issue of concise communication may be more moot than acknowledged presently. At any rate, precise communication appears to trump concise communication in most forensic-clinical circumstances.

Dimensionality may provide a number of distinct general advantages over categorical views. One strength of such a perspective is that it seems to capture and to express a fluid view of sexuality. Sexual or erotic interest and involvement is not a fixed, monolithic entity but appears to shift depending on experience and perhaps more normatively defined "stages" or aspects throughout the course of life. Fixing sexuality may help us as professionals to make limited predictions about the sexual behaviour of clients or research participants, but it likely misses the true nature of sexuality and it is unlikely very helpful to our clients.

Along a related vein, a dimensional approach to sexual offending appears to express the nature of sexual deviation more precisely. If, as reported by a number of investigators (e.g., Abel *et al.*, 1988), there appears to be an

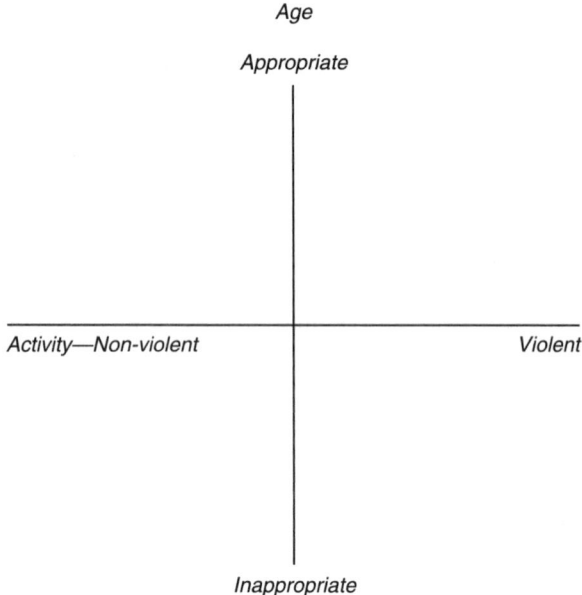

Figure 1.1 Dimensions of sexual offending.

overlap between many sexual offenses – or, in psychiatric parlance, many offenders display multiple paraphilias – it seems likely that offenders can slip easily between various expressions of deviant sexual behaviour. Rather than possessing various, discrete sexual problems, movement could be viewed as more continuous – indeed, effortless – along various continuous dimensions. The appearance of an increasing number of sexual deviations, at least according to the American Psychiatric Association (cf., 1968, 2000), may be just that, an appearance. A close examination of many of the cases presented by Krafft-Ebing (1886/1965) reveals that many of the behaviours attributed to those individuals classified as exhibitionists, for example, appear to have much more in common with other diagnoses. Krafft-Ebing, if not all psychiatric nosologists, likely attempts to force square paraphilic pegs into round holes in order to facilitate a parsimonius nosology but at the expense of an accurate reflection of the state of sexual affairs. Moving individuals or groups around in two- or three-dimensional space is not very difficult, and it may be advantageous if we accept that change via treatment or insight, "spontaneous remission", is possible. It is very possible that such a view of sexual offending will increase the likelihood of such change given that, with our dominant categorical perspective, there is a tendency toward a more pessimistic and static view of offenders. Any change acknowledged is seen as limited. Presently, we treat or attempt to control the symptoms rather than aim for the root of the problem(s). Perhaps part of the difficulty is the stated or unstated assumption that mental health professionals and the public hold concerning the long-term and congenital nature of sexual deviation. A number of my clients have stated as much, and I tend to agree. Sex offenders are, as the quote at the beginning of this chapter illustrates, trying to account for their own deviant behaviour. If we force them to accept attributions of the offensive behaviour that involve genetics, they will view their own efforts at change as futile. By embracing dimensionality, we avoid the tendency to think simplistically and preemptively about sexual offenders. When we use diagnostic labels like pedophilia and exhibitionism, a trap is created that many, professionals and laypersons alike, fall into. Use of a term like pedophilia, a loose and confusing diagnosis at that, leads to viewing the person so labelled as "a pedophile and nothing but a pedophile". The assumed genetic/biological components of this condition reinforce the assumption that there is no hope of recovery or change.

Importantly, too, the unknown and frightening nature of this so-called syndrome leads many to think of people labelled as pedophiles or exhibitionists as Other. "They", very different from "Us", are then less of a threat to those members of the public unused to and likely uncomfortable with issues surrounding sexual abuse and assault. At the same time, however, they become more threatening as Other because they are alien, different, and likely viewed as threatening by possessing stereotyped and monstrous characteristics. Anyone who has inappropriate sexual contact with a minor and is labelled a pedophile is marginalized from the mainstream. Unfortunately, such a move further isolates them from potential help such as informal social support. The social cost of labelling has been noted by some psychologists, even psychologists who engage in serious labelling themselves (e.g., Hare, 1993), but the real cost of labelling is much greater than alienation and ostracism. As a clinician, I have seen the tyranny of labelling regularly in the clients who I have worked with. Men labelled as pedophiles frequently lose hope, and I have probably only met those who have at least a shred of hope remaining because they sought input from me as a psychologist. Many sex offenders are confused and pessimistic about their chances of improvement, obviously not good conditions to begin a long and laborious process of psychotherapy. If one consequence of hopelessness were only suicide or self-harm, many citizens might respond with "Good riddance!" but there is a strong possibility that the response on the part of the offender will be "Screw it! Why should I care about people who don't care about me?" with a resulting increase in lethality in future criminal offenses. Those who really have little concern about themselves because they see little way out of their present untenable circumstances are usually very dangerous individuals. For other reasons as well, including the impact of labelling and the effect on treatability of "diagnosed" offenders, issues to be discussed in later chapters, we should probably avoid categorical views that force "Us" to view "Them" as different and frightening creatures. They are us, and we are them.

Chapter 2

Sexual offender self-labelling and PCT

Most everyone will reject me as a monster . . . I am a failure.
(F. L., incarcerated for the sexual assault of a minor,
personal communication)

"Monster", "failure", "loser", "screw-up", "bastard", and "pervert" are just a few of the labels used by some of my clients convicted of sexual offenses to describe themselves. The quote above is from a Roman Catholic priest who was convicted of the sexual assault on a young male parishioner. This individual, a highly educated and very erudite individual, had serious problems that included a clear sexual preference for prepubescent males and serious issues with substance abuse. The quote contains negative self-statements that I believe are critical in understanding so-called "paraphilias". Any adequate account of sexually deviant behaviour needs to account for the impact of personal experience, labelling, and personal meaning. Rather than positing an imprecise and unknown disease entity to account for sexual perversion, it appears that we can view it as embedded in everyday social interaction and psychosocial processes that occur constantly for each and every one of us. The labels that we apply to ourselves, often the result of repeated labelling by others, can have very real and lasting effects in terms of our actions, both self-directed and other-directed.

Experience, labelling, and construction

The broad camp of constructivism, or constructionism (for a detailed discussion of etymology and epistemology, consult Stam, 1990; Raskin, 2002) appears to provide an answer or set of answers related to meaning, language, and experience. PCT is one constructivistic theory that appears to account for the nature, role, and impact of self-labelling.

One obvious limitation of psychiatric nosological approaches to understanding sexual assault is exclusion of human agency. Autonomy, agency, and choice appear crucial to an adequate explanation of individual social behaviour to many observers (e.g., Weeks, 1995). Individuals tend to be viewed by most areas of psychiatry as slaves to biology – whether genetic or neurological anomalies or biochemical or endocrinological imbalances, we are at the mercy of physiological processes. Even some psychological theories concerned with sexual offenders (e.g., Freud, 1905/1975; Eysenck, 1977) pay little or no attention to choice or will because of their reliance on biology as a strict determinant of human behaviour. Freedom to choose a course of action, based on personal experience, even if the act might be interpreted by the vast majority of observers as "negative" or "undesirable", is not possible or at least not a significant consideration. It would appear to be a grave mistake to argue that biology has absolutely no role to play in any matter sexual, deviant or not, because sex hormones do set broad limits on sexual expression (Hucker and Bain, 1990). What would appear likely is that human biology, rather than determining very specific behavioural expressions, provides changing cues that must be interpreted at various points in an individual's life. While the cues may mean one thing to one person, they might mean a diametrically different thing to another, and a third might choose to ignore the cues altogether as a distraction to a higher concern or calling. Rather than posit a deterministic role for biology, an alternative perspective might be to recognize biology as the mere backdrop against which personal experience is played against.

PCT places important weight on experience and choice. According to Kelly (1955), a person chooses for himself or herself "that alternative in a dichotomized construct through which he anticipates the greater possibility for extension and definition of his system" (p. 64). I would amend this theoretical corollary to include "extension and/or definition of his or her system". What Kelly is concerned with here, and more generally with his theory, are the psychological reasons for particular acts. While this might be referred to as motivation, Kelly (1955, 1958b) chose quite consciously to avoid such a term. For Kelly, to live is to construe, and it is impossible to be a living, breathing human being, at least one not in a vegetative state, and not be "motivated". If everyone is motivated to do something, the notion of motivation has no real significance. This does not mean, however, that we are unable to express concerns about sexual offenders' reasons for doing what they do into PCT terminology. The importance of asking and examining responses to motivational questions, especially for sexual offenders (see Taylor, 1972), has been accepted by many investigators but examined by relatively few.

"Extending a construct system" is one main reason for selecting one act or behaviour. Since all behaviour is experimental, a tentative trial to observe whether an outcome was acceptable or not, having sex with a young boy or assaulting a woman, could allow an individual, as normatively bizarre or repulsive as it may seem, to experience intimacy or potency. It depends, ultimately, on the individual's prior experience and employment of personal constructs, our individual axes of meaning. The extension to an individual's construct system, or psychological processes, does not require any degree of social acceptability, although social demands undoubtedly shape an individual's possible construal of an act before, during, and after the experience. Experience of potency or virility might then lead to confirmation or formation of self-referents such as tough or fearless. In this way, a personal construct system is extended by adding or amending core role construction.

Definition, for Kelly and PCT, refers to more explicit and clear self-definition. The act or repeated acts of forcing a woman to have sex could lead to a more refined sense of self. Whether the self-referent would include a "negative" label such as "rapist", "pervert", or "loser", or whether it would lead to a "positive" label such as "predator", "virile", or "someone no one messes with" probably is a function of the actor's thinking at the time and the immediate social input that they receive. Once adopted, a construct, whether predator or pervert, determines not only future behaviour but future construal patterns and subsequent construct choice. In this way, a channelization of construction can lead an individual down a path involving sexual offenses. The path might prove to be a cul-de-sac eventually, where the individual is cornered figuratively by his or her own constructs. Seeing no other option, an offender might choose suicide or death in a hail of police bullets in order to maintain a personal definition as strong versus weak. Once again, the meaning of the act is not normatively defined but personally defined. From the outside, suicide might always appear "irrational" but, from the inside of a single individual's construct system, suicide might appear the ultimate in rational solutions to an otherwise inescapable corner.

One problem that I have encountered with the idea of choice and agency is the question of freedom, or really the question of limits on freedom. These limits on freedom may be placed by lack of awareness and conditioning. Certainly, when he uses the term "choice", Kelly is not suggesting that individuals have access to all pertinent information before choosing a course of action. We are well aware of limitations on cognitive processing and stated versus actual reasons for behaviour (see Nisbett and Wilson, 1977). We simply cannot know everything about ourselves and the world around us to state categorically and correctly why we choose one act over another. Also, once chosen, we must accept the consequences of an act, and these consequences clearly limit future freedom. An individual does appear free, for whatever conscious or less than conscious reasons, to enact and reenact a wide variety of behaviours, sexually anomalous and offensive ones included. Why, however, would any individual choose the actions of a "creepy pervert"? Why would a person act in a manner that appeared to be both self-injurious and injurious to others? The answer, ultimately, is an individual one in that it depends on his or her own experience and past efforts to construe personal experience and related to self-perceived construct extension and definition. As suggested in Chapter 1, physical injury or humiliation can be self-confirming and hence very positive. Being physically injured and/or humiliated during what one construes as a sexual act can confirm one's identity as a sexual masochist. The pain, in effect, is pleasure for that individual. In the same way, a normative painful or negative label like "baby-fucker" or "rape-hound" can, when reinforced by the experience of molesting babies or raping women, or even being told that one is such a creature, provides a reassurrance in terms of self-identity.

Kelly (1955) and other PCT theorists say little about the origins of constructs, especially as applied to self. The origins of self-referents, negative and otherwise, undoubtedly lie in personal experience. The social environment (e.g., family, peer groups) is responsible no doubt for many of the initial application of these descriptions (see Mead, 1934/1977). Often, my clients convicted of sexual offenses can remember, perhaps because of the emotional impact, an incident in which a parent or school-mate called them sick or perverted. They may have commited some bizarre or troubling act, or may have expressed some strange idea without considering the social context. No doubt acting in an "odd" fashion invites labelling as "odd" by onlookers. More than once I have had a client describe a troubled relationship with a parent, yet, when it came to the final point, conclude something to the effect that "Even though my old man was a bastard, and I hated his guts, he was right about me being a sick fucker who'll never amount to anything." Whatever the particular circumstances, the use of labels by others can lead to internalization. The acceptance of such labels may be instantaneous or very gradual, but the impact and durability of them appears unmistakable. We define ourselves through the feedback or appraisals we receive from other people (Mead, 1934/1977), and sometimes that information is not positive in a normative sense.

There are likely times when we quite consciously adopt a concensus-defined negative descriptor. If part of a subcultural group or gang, especially as a child or youth, we might accept a negative label. "Killer" in many circumstances would be construed as undesirable, but to a youth who has participated in a homicide or gang rape, and has a desire to please friends in a particular deviant peer group or street gang, such a term might be viewed as an honorific title. It is often those around us who define terms, whether normatively or nonnormatively, for us.

On a number of occasions, I have heard from sex offenders that their negative labels, their offensive behaviour, and the wrath and outrage of ordinary citizens are very pleasing to them in that they have accomplished a perverse goal of bringing shame on their own family, a family they despise but have no other means of harming (see Horley, 1995). One client, the son of a very famous and well-to-do individual, stated quite matter of factly that he committed a number of minor and bizarre sexual assaults, usually involving pinching girls and women in very public settings, because he hated his father. He reported that he did not even attempt to elude the police because he wanted to get arrested in order to bring shame on his father, who was an overbearing bully at home according to my client. Such a plan, however perverse, can be effective, and it might actually be accomplished with little personal cost, at least in short-term legal or financial terms. Further negative labels might serve the purpose of reaffirming one's overall negative self-image and, hence, provide a "warm and fuzzy" feeling of self-validation. There is, of course, the possibility that, whatever the original conscious considerations prior to the sexually anomalous behaviour, the origins or true intentions of the actor might well be lost to everyone forever.

According to PCT, the particular labels that we apply to ourselves are known as core constructs, with the particular ways of construing ourselves in a social context as core role constructs (Kelly, 1955). Core role constructs take on an importance that non-self constructions do not share. The ways that we adopt to view ourselves in relation to others, which can be viewed and described in terms of values (Horley, 1991), are difficult to change. Violation of core roles, such as acting in a way unbecoming of a "loyal gang member" or a "merciless predator", produces guilt, and the experience of imminent, comprehensive core change in general will result in threat and, likely, resistance (Kelly, 1955; see especially Winter, 1992a). Core constructs, and core role constructs in particular, are not readily altered.

Over the years of my clinical work with sex offenders, I have found that much of the work that I do concerns challenging existing personal labels. Pointed questions about the nature of particular core constructs can begin the long process of construct redefinition or reassignment of self with respect to these notions. The labels may be formal ones, such as "psychopath" or "homosexual pedophile", applied by well-intentioned mental health professionals. Those professionals who write popular books on sexual offenders (e.g., Salter, 2003) are a source of some of these constructs. Unquestionably, the terms may be more informal or colloquial ones, such as "asshole" or "freak" provided by less well-intentioned antagonists. More often than not, the antagonists include criminal associates, other inmates, and prison guards. However the label is acquired, the task of questionning the user of such labels appears worthwhile. Many sex offenders accept personal labels quite freely in an attempt to interpret their own bewildering and harmful acts. Many of these self-referents, as tentative and fuzzy as they may be, only appear to hinder or exacerbate the situation, making reoffense more likely. Some formal professional labels are adopted with little knowledge of their general meaning. The individual who accepts such a label from an authority figure might not even ask about the meaning of the term, perhaps to avoid the appearance of ignorance, yet they will do their own "research" into the definition and implications of the term. Personal investigations might take them to other individuals so labelled, or to confidants who may have little understanding of the term themselves.

My questions about the personal meanings of many self-referents, especially formal ones like bisexual pedophile, have brought many interesting responses. A common response is a look of disbelief and a question (e.g., "What, don't you know?", "Aren't you supposed to be the psychologist?"). Another common response is a blank facial expression and a brief summary of bewilderment (e.g., "I dunno."). Some clients, either overcoming any doubts they have about my own professional deficits or seeing themselves responsible for informing me about some condition that I probably should know something about, provide very elaborate definitions and descriptions of various conditions that they quite clearly possess. At times, the definitions are textbook perfect; at times, they are confused and conflated with other terminology. If I follow my first question with a second more probing one (e.g., "So do think you have that disorder/condition/disease?"), a common reply is a simple shoulder shrug. A second frequent response is hostility and anger. No doubt, in addition to seeming a simpleton to some, I am a bothersome pest to other men who simply want some clear "truth" about the nature of their conditions. Quite interestingly, a few individuals, who are possibly questioning the nature of their diagnostic or formal labels, are quite prepared to accept that the label is a professional construct applied by another that does not really describe them. I have seen symptoms disappear relatively quickly when the possibility is raised that the label is someone else's construction. Some symptoms may well be, in a sense, extensions of the diagnostic process whereby an individual concludes that, if the label is to fit, the various symptoms must be present. While this may occur in a small minority of cases, it certainly raises important questions about the impact of the traditional psychodiagnostic process. These are issues and concerns that have been discussed by other writers (e.g., Raskin and Epting, 1993; Honos-Webb and Leitner, 2001) and need not be reproduced here.

It appears important for individuals to assume responsibility for their own behaviour in spite of personal trauma and damaging experience (Kelly, 1969; Honos-Webb and Leitner, 2001). It is important, too, that they are not forced to shoulder the demands of others' constructions of them. What is needed is support, guidance, and some insights into existing constructs, and possible alternatives, that would allow these individuals to re-create themselves. If we grant ourselves creative and re-creative powers, why not grant the same abilities to sexual offenders?

Essentialist arguments in the realm of sexuality in general, and perverse sexuality in particular, do not seem to hold (Kinsman, 1991; Weeks, 1995). Any medico-scientific position that maintains certain immutable and transcultural features to sexual expression is misguided. Sexuality and those aspects of ourselves that we can construe as sexual are creations of experience, both public and private. The denial or at least diminution of personal experience and choice by the medico-scientific approach has a very serious impact on a key component in altering sexually offensive behaviour, namely responsibility. True, a medical diagnosis and treatment prescription, possibly in the form of long-term anti-androgen medication, requires some responsibility on the part of the "patient", but it is usually limited to attending medical appointments and complying with medication schedules. The real responsibility for change lies with the medical professionals, or perhaps the multinational pharmaceutical firms, in providing some form of efficacious treatment. At this point in time, it is often said to sexual offenders that "there is no cure for your condition, only control of symptoms". The "afflicted" individual is, hence, rendered relatively passive and dependent.

Another consequence of the medico-scientific view of sex offenders is loss of hope on the part of the offender (see quote at the beginning of this chapter). This is a very serious and unfortunate problem. Hope for improvement is a critical component, yet it is easily lost or set aside when a person is told that his or her affliction is possibly genetic or at least longstanding (Honos-Webb and Leitner, 2001). Hope is diminished further when the client is told that there are no or few effective existing treatments. Without hope, why carry on, or why attempt to change? Acceptance of one's present state of affairs, however undesirable, seems the best possible outcome unless other drastic measures (e.g., suicide) are considered. Hope, I believe, is offered by PCT in reconstruction of existing conceptual structures, although the false hope of easy, immediate alteration and elimination of unwanted behaviour must be avoided.

If we are concerned, as we should be, with the personal constructs of sexual offenders, what do we know at this point about such constructs? While research in PCT proper has been limited to date, enough research in the field of sexual offending has been conducted to allow us to search relatively disparate areas, including sociology and beyond the narrow boundaries of forensic mental health research, to examine the findings.

Sex offender constructs: a review of the research

The role that fantasy plays in deviant sexuality in general and child molestation in particular was examined by Marshall (1973). Marshall showed that an attempt to control and alter the deviant sexual fantasies of five child molesters was effective in reducing penile responses to child stimuli as well as inappropriate sexual behavior outside the treatment setting. Marshall (see Marshall and Barbaree, 1988) has included alteration of deviant fantasies in a treatment program for child molesters. Abel and Blanchard (1974), too, demonstrated the centrality of deviant fantasy, as have others (e.g., MacCullough et al., 1983). Perhaps first and foremost, fantasies serve as "try-outs" or "experimental planning" (MacCulloch et al., 1983). Lanyon (1986) and Quinsey (1986) have concluded that an account of sexual fantasy is essential for any adequate explanation of child molestation, and examination of fantasy is an important component of any effective treatment program.

Abel et al. (1984) have investigated the role that certain beliefs and attitudes play in continued sexual involvement by adults with children. They have focussed in particular on seven types of beliefs about children and sex that they term "cognitive distortions". These distorted beliefs include: if children fail to resist advances, they must want sex; sexual activity with children is an appropriate means to increase the sexual knowledge of the children; if children fail to report sexual activity, they must condone it; in the future, sex between adults and children will be acceptable if not encouraged; if one fondles rather than penetrates, sex with children is acceptable; any children who ask questions about sex really desire it; and one can develop a close relationship with a child through sexual contact. According to Abel *et al.*, the commonality among all of these "wrong" views (i.e., inappropriate insofar as children cannot consent meaningfully to sexual interaction) is that child molesters make no attempt to validate them against the experience of others. A number of writers confirm that child molesters do report these and similar sexual attitudes and beliefs about children. Stermac and Segal (1989), for example, reported that child molesters, compared to normals, perceive more benefits for children as a result of adult sexual contact, greater complicity on the child's part, and less responsibility on the adult's part. Hayashino *et al.* (1995) used a shortened version of the Abel *et al.* Cognition Scale to show that extrafamilial molesters, compared to non-offenders and even incest offenders, report more distorted cognitions.

Whether the full or modified Cognition Scale, there appear to be some limitations of this device. Horley and Quinsey (1995) failed to find any hypothesized differences using Abel's Cognition Scale because of high top-end loading. Because of the transparency of the items, all expressed very negatively but scored in the reverse, incarcerated molesters in particular may be reluctant to report distortions. This concern and others (see Ward *et al.*, 1997a) led Bumby (1996) to develop a 38-item MOLEST Scale. This assessment of cognitive distortions in child molesters is similar to the Cognition Scale, but items appear to be much more "neutral" in tone (e.g., "Some children can act very seductively.") and may avoid problems encountered by some of those using the Cognition Scale. Preliminary psychometric reports of the internal and test-retest reliabilities of the MOLEST Scale, as well as convergent and discriminative validities, are encouraging (Bumby, 1996), but it is premature to endorse this scale without reservation. Collings (1997) too has developed a 15-item scale to examine child sexual abuse myths, or really distorted beliefs or cognitions. Again, initial psychometric data for his CSA scale are quite adequate, but further efforts are demanded.

Although studies of the attributional processes per se of child molesters are few in number, some sociological and social psychological investigation has examined beliefs and what could be termed social cognition. McCaghy (1967, 1968) showed that the amount of coercion in the sexual activity with children predicted level of denial and attempts to maintain an identity as "sexually normal". Interestingly, he also found that, although incarceration and probation had no significant impact on motivational change, the number of psychotherapeutic sessions did affect self-confessed motives. After 11 individual or 21 group sessions (McCaghy, 1967), or roughly 20 sessions of unspecified therapy (McCaghy, 1968), child molesters tended to accept more personal responsibility for their actions, as opposed to blaming an alcohol or drug problem. They also tended to provide many "psychodynamic" explanations for their behaviour, not surprisingly given the psychoanalytic orientation of most of their therapists, past and present. McCaghy (1968) warned, however, that the label "child molester" should be avoided lest offenders come to accept such a deviant role as an integral part of themselves.

Taylor (1972) had judges sort motivational accounts into categories on a scale from "likely to be true" to "unlikely to be true". He found that the sexual offenders themselves invoked "mental breakdown" reasons for their behaviour much more often than "social skill deficit" explanations. Judges, however, rated "social skill deficit" reasons as more credible than "mental breakdown" reasons. These patterns of attribution, with minimization and denial of deviance, appear consistent with clinical findings concerning offenders' use of denial and minimization (Barbaree, 1989).

Ward et al. (1993) had incarcerated child molesters complete an attribution scale at three points in time while describing and explaining their most recent sexual offense. They found that sexual needs were reported by far most often, followed by intimacy needs, especially during their recall of the lapse (stage two) just prior to their sexual assault. Along similar lines, Ward et al. (1995b) examined molesters' accounts of the chain of thoughts and feelings that accompanied their most recent offenses. The resulting qualitative data led them to propose a nine-stage process for child molesters' offense chains that emphasized distorted beliefs. Earlier, Ward et al. (1994) found that child molesters who reported a lapse viewed the causes of their deviant behaviour as more uncontrollable than molesters without a lapse.

Child molesters' attitudes have been examined by some investigators. The technique of choice has been the semantic differential technique, first presented by Osgood et al. (1957). Marks and Sartorius (1967) argued that sexual attitude is an important component in the assessment and treatment of sexual deviation, and they presented a "sexualized" version of the semantic differential. Their technique included not only bipolar adjectives that Osgood et al. would classify as general evaluative (e.g., kind–cruel, good–bad), but they included sexual evaluative adjectives as well (e.g., seductive–repulsive, erotic–frigid). Factor analysis of the assessment device showed that there was some distinction between the general and sexual evaluative scales, although the two factors were similar. In an examination of the clinical utility of the technique with eight clients who revealed a variety of sexual deviations, they found that attitude change paralleled clinical change. They concluded, therefore, that their version of the semantic differential provided "useful indicators of clinical progress" (p. 448). For a concise clinical tool, they recommended an abbreviated version of their technique with three sexual evaluative (viz., sexy–sexless, seductive–repulsive, and erotic–frigid) and three general evaluative scales (viz., kind–cruel, good–bad, and pleasant–unpleasant).

Quinsey *et al.* (1976) used this brief sexual semantic differential as part of their test battery in a study of change in child molesters over the course of an aversion therapy program. Together with significant pre-treatment versus post-treatment changes in penile plethysmographic responses and skin conductance responses, Quinsey *et al.* found that the general evaluative and sexual evaluative scales were highly correlated and that both showed the expected interaction of increased ratings for adults and decreased ratings for children, in line with both penile circumference and skin conductance results. Thus, the semantic differential appears to be a useful paper-and-pencil measure of attitudes that are relevant to the treatment of child molestation. One warning sounded later by Quinsey (1977, 1986), however, concerns the transparency of any devices that include only sex-related dimensions. The ability of respondents, many of whom are highly motivated to dissemble, to appear as they wish to be seen should not be overlooked.

Another application of the semantic differential with child molesters was provided by Frisbie and colleagues (Frisbie *et al.*, 1967; Dingman *et al.*, 1968). They described the general technique as "non-threatening" and "relatively ambiguous" (Frisbie *et al.*, 1967, p. 700). They argued further that it and similar psychological assessment techniques are important "because an adult male's selection of a child as a sexual object seems to be related to his perceptions of the self, his role in a given social structure, and his recognition and/or acceptance of ethical values and social expectations" (p. 699). Their research involved an examination of incarcerated and released child molesters' views of themselves and their ideal selves. One bipolar adjective pair, "happy–sad", was found to distinguish incarcerated from community molesters, with community molesters reporting more resemblance between their actual versus ideal selves on this dimension than incarcerated offenders. This finding in part led to the conclusion that released offenders were "better integrated" than incarcerated offenders, but Frisbie *et al.* correctly noted that this could be a reflection of their different situations rather than personality differences. A one-year follow-up of 79 of the released molesters (Dingman *et al.*, 1968) showed that the respondents' views of both their real and ideal selves declined. This finding was described in terms of erosion of morale, and it was related to concern about impending recidivism.

Borrowing from Marks and Sartorius (1967), Frisbie *et al.* (1967) and Horley and Quinsey (1994) developed a semantic differential to examine child molesters' attitudes or thoughts about themselves and other individuals. Child molesters, relative to non-molesters, described themselves as submissive and sexually unattractive, while they described women as oppressive and unattractive. Examination of the child molester group alone revealed some intragroup differences using Kelly's (1955) role construct repertory grid (rep grid). Responses of molesters who had exclusively victimized girls included significantly more external appearance constructs, while offenders against young boys used more emotional and self-sufficiency terms to describe people. Molesters who had killed their young victims described men and boys as cruel but sexy. Untreated molesters reported more social anxiety than treated offenders (Horley and Quinsey, 1995). A subsequent study (Horley et al., 1997), using a revised semantic differential, confirmed that molesters described themselves as less positive sexually than did non-molesters. Women were seen by molesters more negatively in terms of sexual descriptors than by non-molesters although, somewhat paradoxically, molesters described women as more trusting and mature than non-molesters. Molesters also reported a more positive view of women on the Attitudes Toward Women Scale (Nelson, 1988) than comparison participants. Molesters and non-molesters also differed in terms of their responses to the Criminal Sentiments Scale (Andrews and Wormith, 1990), with child molesters reporting a more favourable view of the police, courts, and legal process than comparison participants. A similar finding was revealed in ratings of authority figures: child molesters described authorities as kinder and less repulsive, deceitful, and unpleasant than comparisons. Marshall et al. (2003) found that this semantic differential did not differentiate between child molesters, non-sex offenders, and community-based non-offenders with respect to views of women and children. It is important to note, however, that Marshall et al. modified our original semantic differential for their research and did not use the Horley et al. (1997) modified scale.

A modest but potentially significant study by Howells (1979) examined the thoughts of child molesters and offenders without sexual offenses concerning people in their social environments in terms of personal constructs. Howells compared the personal constructs of ten "mentally disordered", heterosexual child molesters and ten non-sex offenders using versions of the rep grid. The constructs elicited from Howells' respondents were sorted according to an amended version of Landfield's (1971) categorization scheme, and analyses revealed certain differences between offender groups. Perhaps most importantly, child molesters used more "egoistic" constructs, such as "domineering–passive" and "dominant–submissive", than non-molesters. Children were described generally as passive and submissive. There was also a suggestion that molesters were concerned with small body parts such as small genitalia. A combination of both offender groups, where constructs elicited using male and female elements were compared, showed that women were construed in terms of sexual and physical appearance while men were interpreted in terms of status and organization.

Wilson and Cox (1983a, 1983b) provided some indirect support for Howells' (1979) egoism finding. In a study of the personality of 77 members of a British child molester organization, Wilson and Cox (1983a) found that child molesters frequently described themselves as shy and attracted to children because of the children's naive innocence. They concluded that dominance was a key to understanding a man's choice of a child as a sexual partner.

A conceptual replication of Howells' work was attempted by Horley (1988a), who compared the personal constructs of ten "mentally disordered", mixed (heterosexual and homosexual) child molesters and ten "mentally disordered" non-sex offenders. Analyses confirmed the previous findings concerning the tendency of the combined groups to think of women, compared to men, in terms of sexual and physical appearance, but the egoistic construct difference between groups was not found. Neither did there seem to be a preoccupation with small body size among child sexual abusers. The failure to replicate the between-group egoism finding may be due to differences between the two studies (e.g., heterosexual versus mixed molesters, prison comparison versus mental health comparison), but it is also possible that the original egoism finding is attributable to statistical artifact.

More recently, Marshall and colleagues (e.g., Marshall and Mazzucco, 1995) have pointed to a related concern with the self-perception and self-esteem of child molesters. Low self-esteem does appear to be a consequence of the actions of child molesters in terms of impact on their victims (Freshwater et al., 2001), but Marshall and colleagues have argued that low self-esteem leads adult males to seek sexual relationships with children. Certainly some child molesters report negative self-feelings, and this may help to explain their offending (Ward et al., 1993). Ward et al. (1997b) also reported low self-esteem among molesters, although one study by Marshall et al. (2003) did not find that child molesters' self-esteem differed significantly from comparisons. Horley et al. (1997) suggested that the situation may be more complex, in that child molesters may perceive themselves as inadequate sexually, or not very physically attractive, but they are not low in self-esteem generally. At least two studies with incarcerated molesters appear to support this view (Horley and Quinsey, 1994; Horley et al., 1997). This issue has yet to be settled.

A valuable study by Johnston et al. (1997) examined the "sexual thoughts" (i.e., words relevant to children and/or sexual activity) of incarcerated child molesters, in particular their ability to suppress unwanted or inappropriate thoughts. They concluded that there is both "some hope and some notes of caution" (p. 303) after showing that sexual thoughts could be suppressed but more so by situational offenders than obsessed molesters. They also concluded that thought suppression techniques alone are insufficient for changing child molesters' inappropriate behaviour.

The empirical literatures concerned with child molesters' cognitions have been expanding, especially over the past two decades. At this point, very little of substance can be concluded safely. Certainly fantasy, particularly deviant sexual fantasy, appears to be an important factor in producing and maintaining child molestation. Alteration of deviant fantasy is an important target in many treatment programs designed for child molesters. Cognitive distortions as described by Abel, Bumby, and others do appear to be factors, but whether they are causes, effects, or co-occurances of molestation is unknown. Indeed, how many molesters who hold what types of unacceptable beliefs is not known. Whether certain types of distorted beliefs about sexuality are more "serious" (i.e., are more likely to lead to sexually offensive behaviour) than others remains unanswered as well. The adequacy of some of the techniques we use to assess beliefs, attitudes, values, distorted cognitions, personal constructs, or any number of other cognitive propositions, processes, or products is certainly open to question too. Doubts have been raised about the usefulness of the Cognition Scale, but more work needs to be done on alternatives (e.g., MOLEST Scale, CSA Scale). The semantic differential and rep grid are two methods, as opposed to specific scales, that have been used in a variety of studies but, because they represent general methodological approaches, specific content needs to be identified. To do this, more informed "hunches" or clinical insights are needed. The lack of overarching theory or general theoretical insights, however, is a limitation here.

The question of child molesters' thoughts about themselves, particularly concerning self-worth and self-esteem, is very much that: a question. Child molesters may see themselves as undesirable or less than adequate individuals, as Marshall and Mazzucco (1995) would argue, but molesters may only perceive and report a lack of attractiveness or sexual adequacy, and even this might be more true for molesters with male victims rather than female victims. It may also be true only for certain incarcerated offenders. Whatever the case, negative self-image may provide the basis for the relatively consistent behavioural finding that many child molesters display or report shyness or difficulty in social interaction (Quinsey, 1986; Salter, 1988). The importance of assessing and altering thoughts about inadequacy or lack of social/sexual efficacy is indicated. At this point, it seems clear that most if not all child molesters hold some distorted cognitions or beliefs about adult–child sex or what constitute appropriate relationships with children. The problem is that this appears to be the case almost by definition. The specific types of distortion, or the degrees of risk associated with various distorted views are unknown. The types of distorted cognition by types of offender (e.g., male versus female victim, amount of force or sadistic behaviour in assault) demand examination. Assessment development in this area appears important whether one is interested specifically in distorted cognitions, beliefs, values, or fantasies. Use of the Cognition Scale, particularly with incarcerated offenders, seems limited by narrow focus and construction. The MOLEST Scale or CSA Scale may prove better, but again they may be too narrow in design.

Social cognitive research into child molesters' attributional processes has found, not surprisingly, that molesters tend to have difficulty accounting for their sexually deviant behaviour. Many ascribe their offenses to alcohol abuse. In sociological terms, their deviance disavowal is understandable as an attempt to appear more normal sexually than they in fact behave. More detailed studies examining differences among molesters need to be done. Such work may reveal, for example, that practicing heterosexual males who molest young boys need to engage in more "mental gymnastics", and experience more accompanying anxiety, in order to explain themselves because they have more perceived deviance to disavow or to account for. Assessment of causal attributions of sexually inappropriate behaviour is helpful in programming, and it serves as a specific therapeutic target in treatment.

Relatively little work has been done with men who assault adults sexually, perhaps reflecting the lack of interest by psychiatry in rape (APA, 2000), although some interesting suggestions and empirical research relevant to rapists' constructions have been presented. Men who assault women have been found to have views supportive of the "rape myths" (e.g., women desire rape), and this may increase a likelihood of using force during a sexual encounter (Stermac et al., 1990). Stermac et al. also discussed the role of a sense of hostility toward women that many men who assault adult females report.

Shorts (1985) reported on a single rapist who, over the course of therapy in a forensic hospital, came to view himself as more like men who assault women. His distance from women, however, in terms of both self and ideal self was significant at the beginning and end of treatment. This may reflect what Malamuth (1984) has described as "hostile masculinity", or a very patronizing and aggressive "machismo", on the part of men who rape. One problem in attempting to understand the constructions of rapists, however, is the tendency, like Malamuth, to generalize as if all rapists share common features. On the same lines, Rada (1978) argued that rapists suffer from what he termed the "Madonna–Prostitute Complex", or a tendency to think in extreme terms of women as either extremely pure, and not to be touched, or extremely impure, and to be touched whenever desired. Carnahan (1987) investigated this hypothesis using a form of rep grid with incarcerated rapists. He could find no overall support, although he did find that rapists viewed rape victims as "less pure" than did incarcerated property offenders. Carnahan's sample included only rapists who had been sentenced to confinement of two years or less, and it is possible that a group of more serious or repeat offenders might show more extreme construal patterns. Again, the problem with the limited work on rapists to date, however, is the tendency to view all rapists as having common constructions. In fact, Prentky and Knight (1991) have demonstrated that there are many different subtypes of rapists with different "motives" defining each.

Some first-time violent offenders, especially assaultive individuals, may act to validate essentially invalid predictions (Houston, 1998). Many repeat violent offenders, however, act in line with self-related constructs and views of others that involve aggressive or violent labels (Needs, 1988). Gang violence, in particular, may be the "cement" by which individuals establish a group identity for themselves. Specific forms of violent offense have been examined by a number of investigators. Howells (1983) administered repertory grids to a number of violent offenders deemed to be "mentally disordered" (see Houston, 1998). He found that repeat offenders compared to first offenders saw themselves in a more positive light despite, or perhaps because of, their lengthy criminal histories. Needs (1988), too, found that a repeatedly violent offender saw himself in a positive manner (for example, "wild" as opposed to "soft"). Landfield (1971), however, found evidence that some violent offenders do not construe violence positively. One violent individual saw many people as violent and unhappy, including himself, and lashed out impulsively to perceived offenses of others. This individual was a severe alcoholic, however, which may have a significant impact on his construal of self and others. A case of an arsonist (Landfield, 1971) was similarly intriguing in that the arsonist had a very tight construct system with themes of religion and morality, and generally saw herself as a good and God-fearing person, but may well have shifted to the "bad, Devilish" view when unable to keep to her very high standards. The arsonist examined by Fransella and Adams (1966), too, was a very religious individual. Horley and Quinsey (1995) found differences between child molesters who kill victims compared with those who do not in that child killers viewed men as more cruel and stronger than those who did not kill. One problem with these and other studies of violent offenders is that they involve very different expressions of violence. If we accept that specific types of sexual offenders are heterogeneous, no doubt violent offenders cannot be considered a single group. More consideration of the specific nature of the violence, such as assault or homicide, is required in further research.

There are a variety of other forms of sexual deviation, commonly classed as "nuisance" offenses because of a lack of physical contact or at least less physical trauma inflicted on victims. In general, in part because they are viewed as less severe offenses, we know little about the offenders in general – they tend to not be incarcerated for long periods when discovered and adjudicated, and they tend not to step forward on their own for treatment – and very little work from a PCT perspective has been done.

Men who exhibit their genitalia for sexual gratification, so-called exhibitionists (APA, 1994), are seldom studied despite very high offense rates (Mohr et al., 1964). Landfield and Epting (1987) reported on a single exhibitionist who, when completing a rep grid, had difficulty nominating acquaintances, especially women, for specific role titles. Whether this is a common circumstance of these individuals, and whether it is precursor or effect of the problem, is unknown. One partially successful treatment that I (Horley, 1995) conducted with a repeat exhibitionist showed that this individual viewed himself as a "pervert" who repeatedly offended in part to strike back at his family. To argue that such a personal construct is at the basis of all exhibitionism is premature and facile. Much more research with these offenders is required.

Those individuals who observe others unknowingly, usually disrobing or engaging in sexual activity, for sexual gratification purposes, or voyeurs

(APA, 1994), are especially difficult to study (i.e., rarely incarcerated or hospitalized). My clients over the years who have engaged in this type of behaviour have never been specialists. They have had some other form of sexual deviance, either exhibitionism or obscene telephone calling, and this pattern has been reported elsewhere (Abel *et al.*, 1988). My only insight into this sexual deviation is that these men, who view themselves as "normal" by noting that anyone who consumes "adult" media or who attends "exotic" shows is voyeuristic, admit to timidity when approaching potential sexual partners. Whether this is the result of a desire for "intimidating" partners or a perceived social deficiency on their parts is not clear.

Certainly a number of more exotic forms of sexual deviance, such as frotteurism (APA, 1994), or the public rubbing against other individuals for sexual gratification, have been examined, albeit infrequently, and rarely from a PCT perspective. In the case of frotteurism, I (Horley, 2000) have argued that the few "frotteurs" that I have worked with over the years make me wonder about the need for a separate diagnostic category, since these individuals appear to be timid, would-be rapists. If only to deny a convenient "medical escape", we should limit such labels until we have more information about the nature of the distinct problem.

Can we make any general comments or draw any general conclusions about the nature of sexual offenders' personal constructs? Are their subtypes of sexual offenders who seem to subscribe to a particular set of constructs that lead to sexually aberrant behaviour? At this point in time, it appears far too premature to draw any definitive conclusions, but we may have some findings that will bear up under further exploration and examination. While not concerned with personal constructs per se, fantasy can be viewed as an important part of the cognitive rehearsal process based on construction, and it appears to be an important component in the sexual enactment of offenders. Not everyone who has violent sexual fantasies will necessarily act on them, but it is an indicator that should be taken seriously for those who have a history of sexual violence. Interest in non-sexual violence has been found to be a predictor of violent reoffense (Quinsey *et al.*, 1998), and any report or finding of an interest or fantasy involving the inflicting of extreme suffering should be taken seriously.

Men who engage in sex with prepubescent children may construe children as non-dominant or non-domineering, as opposed to adults, who are so demanding as to cause anxiety and, ultimately, repulsion. This interpretation, however, may well only apply to men who abuse young girls as opposed to boys. At this point, this and other findings are very difficult to accept as definitive because many of the studies are single research efforts.

While more research is demanded, there are limitations with the direction of the existing research. One problem concerns the limited concerns of the research to date. Almost all research involves incarcerated sexual offenders, and there is no doubt that the adjudication process and the experience of incarceration have important impacts on personal construct systems. Also, most research on sex offenders deals only with construct content rather than the structure of construing (Winter, 1992a). Examination of the manner in which constructs are employed by individuals is required before an in-depth understanding of sex offenders' construal processes can be achieved. Perhaps more importantly, much of the research to date has been nomothetic (i.e., based on the analysis of grouped data). A truly idiographic approach along the lines suggested originally by Kelly (1955) would direct more attention at the individual case and analyze the individual before aggregating the findings. This does not limit one to simple case studies since any form of therapeutic or social intervention can provide a manipulation or independent variable for an experimental study. There are certainly examples within the PCT literature on sex offenders of just such single-case experiments (e.g., Horley, 2005), and these reports should not be dismissed as "mere case studies". It appears, however, that we need to focus more on individuals in terms of further research in order to clarify the nature of constructs and construct usage by sex offenders who are unique in some ways, as indeed all are. Only then should we move on to more grouped data of offenders who seem to share some important characteristic (e.g., interest in prepubescent males only, rubbing against adult females in public places). In subsequent chapters of this book, despite some discussions that will be necessarily general, the focus of discussion will be the single case and specific individuals.

Chapter 3

Social power and sexual assault

> I don't feel good about my preference for children and it depresses me quite a bit because of what I do. Feel powerless/helpless because of the media's claim, generally, that it is "incurable" and there's no hope for someone such as I that has this condition.
>
> (R. P., incarcerated for the sexual assault of a prepubescent male, personal communication)

One important consideration with respect to sexual assault concerns the centrality of social power in the commission of the offense. According to Brownmiller (1975), Darke (1990), and other writers, sexual assault is essentially about power and control and not due to a need for sexual gratification. Brownmiller's important book, *Against our will,* is a critique of patriarchy from a radical feminist perspective. Through an examination of the various ways, across both culture and time, that men have committed sexual assault, Brownmiller concludes that sexual assault is a means by which men oppress women. Sexual assault, whether an individual man attacking one woman or a conquering army employing rape systematically to denigrate thousands of women, is simply one means by which men attain and maintain social dominance. There certainly appears to be support for this position; for example, a sizeable minority, if not majority of men who assault women sexually are unable to achieve penile penetration and use other means (e.g., hands, gun barrels) to commit the offense. The issue, however, does not appear quite so clearcut, and questions need to be raised. If sex is really unimportant, why do so many assaults have a clear central sexual component? Would not a sexual component, however effective at adding humiliation and degradation to the assault, impede the use of force or more direct means of domination? Does not the sexual component leave the attacker at risk or more vulnerable than, say, a physical beating would? Unfortunately, very few recent researchers and writers have addressed directly the issues raised by Brownmiller and colleagues about the importance of social power, and this appears necessary.

One stumbling block in discussions of social power concerns a common understanding, or an acceptable definition, of power. Social power can be relatively straightforward insofar as both sociological and psychological sources are concerned so long as the essence of the term rather than the particulars are the real focus. Weber (1947/1964), from a macro sociological perspective, defined power as "the probability that one actor within a social relationship will be in a position to carry out his own will despite resistance, regardless of the basis on which the probability rests" (p. 152). According to Weber, it is the ability to gain social compliance in the face of resistance that is the essence of power. Psychologists tend to be concerned with the individual, the micro-level concerns, and the social impact of one individual on another. For psychologists (e.g., Minton, 1967; Ng, 1980), power is more about the ability of an individual to change the thoughts, feelings, and/or behaviours of another individual against the desires of the second individual. Key and common elements from both the macro and micro levels are the ability to change, or gain compliance to demands, involving social players and opposition to that change. Thus, despite differences in focus and terminology, both disciplines share a core concern about social power.

Power is very much a part of all social relations. Unfortunately, especially in psychology, it is all too often ignored or excluded from the discussion. The only time that it may enter discussions about relationships is in extreme cases of exploitation or "evil". Power, however, appears as a necessary aspect of all considerations of social interaction insofar as all social actors or entities are not equal, and we need to account for differences among social elements. Relationships are shaped by a variety of factors, and it is important to include an analysis of power when considering social relations. In a very real manner, power refers to a relational characteristic between individuals or any social entities (Wrong, 1979; Willutzki and Duda, 1996) despite a tendency in psychology to attribute power as a characteristic of individuals (see Minton, 1967). According to May (1972), any specific characteristics or dispositions of individuals might best be described as strengths. Although a person can possess physical strength because of muscular development, or a nation can possess military strength due to advanced weaponry, power is only a relevant consideration when such an attribute is presented, either directly or indirectly, when two or more players engage in a social exchange. These attributes may also be misrepresented by one or both parties, insofar as muscles or weapons of mass destruction may be less than indicated or not exist at all. Whatever the actual, imagined, or officially listed nature of the strengths, they help to define the nature of the relationship. The individual or larger social entity with the power directs the relationship in terms of particular ends (e.g., meals served on time and in silence, favourable terms in bilateral trade agreements).

A focus of the discussion in the context of sex offenders is the misuse of power. Power employed to assist people is not at issue here, but power employed to exploit, oppress, or abuse people is very much in question. In a sense, abuse of power is at the basis of all criminal offending, whether involving property or people, insofar as criminal activity demands outcomes and expects victims to comply with those demands because of strengths or advantages possessed by offenders. We could and perhaps should wonder now about the nature of the advantage possessed by the powerful, and the power bases used by those who have power, especially sexual offenders.

Bases of power and control

Many social scientists, especially psychologists, who write on power frequently consider only limited aspects of the sources of social power. French and Raven (1953), for example, presented a good discussion of a number of power bases from a psychosocial perspective, but their discussion was limited to only the use of power by authority. While authority is an important source of power conferred by society, it is far from the only source. It is, however, a good starting point for a consideration of power bases, and Wrong (1979), a sociologist who has provided a classic overview of the complex nature of social power, presented a good framework for such a consideration.

Authority refers to formal, established, and accepted roles and relationships within a social context. According to Wrong (1979), we need to consider five important bases of power by authority: coercive, induced, legitimate, competent, and personal. Although the terms are somewhat different, these are in essence the same bases presented earlier by French and Raven (1953). Coercive authority gains compliance via the use of punishment. If you do not do as ordered by the authority, either an individual (e.g., a policeman on the street) or a much larger social entity (e.g., a central government committee), something unpleasant or aversive will occur. The punishment might be a nominal fine imposed by a local court or perhaps a death sentence via state-ordered execution. Induced authority, on the other hand, bases its control on the use of payment. A pleasant result, whether a tasty snack to eat or a massive business contract from a government, is used as inducement for compliance with demands. Legitimate authority is more subtle. It is based on established norms and expectations. Compliance is the result of an unquestioning and common understanding of tradition or "the rules" (e.g., "That's just the way we do things here."). Competent authority possesses power based on specialized knowledge or skill that directs compliance (e.g., "As your physician, I direct you to take that medication."). Finally, personal authority finds power in a "personal" relationship based on love for or the charismatic nature of the authority figure. Compliance is based on the degree of the personal attachment (e.g., "As your beloved television evangelist, I command that you viewers mail in every last penny you have.").

Just as authority has multiple bases or sources of power, non-authority-based power is multifaceted. There are three further bases of power beyond authority, at least according to Wrong (1979), and these are force, persuasion, and manipulation. Force refers to physical force, and it is clear that the application of physical force is not the only effective means by which compliance is achieved. Threats of the use of force, such as "Shut-up or I'll punch you!" or "If you do not surrender your country, our armed forces will crush you!", are probably very effective means of gaining compliance in certain circumstances. It might also be the case that force is implied by the issue of a particular order or demand that typically is supported by a particular level of force (e.g., "That little guy wouldn't demand the money from me as a store owner if he didn't have a gun or some weapon!").

Persuasion is a source of power in that prolonged discussion can bring about compliance if rational argumentation is brought to bear on a social situation. In this case, the social players know what is at stake, and understand the nature of the non-compliant action, but communicate in order to attempt to change the situation. The "silver-tongued devil" possesses power to the extent that compliance is achieved via "straight talk" about the benefits of doing or thinking what is requested. Manipulation, on the other hand, is the use of techniques to gain compliance when the outcome is not made clear to the victim, or at least the intended victim. Manipulation can take many different forms, both personal and social, and both individuals and social institutions can become "masters of manipulation" in order to gain compliance and achieve goals.

One power base that has not been discussed by any source that I am aware of is extortion. An extortionist – again, either a single individual or a larger social entity – achieves compliance by the uses of goods or information that can be used to produce compliance by the mere threat of use or possibly the brief demonstration of the capacity to do damage. In this way, it differs from both persuasion, where the weight of socially defined reasonable argument is used to gain a known outcome, and manipulation, where a number of tactics can be used to gain an outcome unknown to the intended target. Criminal extortion, more commonly known as blackmail, describes a process by which an extortionist threatens to reveal materials depicting criminal or embarrassing activities unless some payment is made to keep the material secret. Extortion can happen on a grand scale in the world of international relations (e.g., demanding cooperation in a trade deal or else certain information will be released to the media that could cripple an economy). In the realm of interpersonal relations, however, extortion can involve the threat of revealing information best left private (e.g., "You'd better be nice to me or I'll tell everyone what you did last summer."). It can also involve the threat or use of emotional blackmail (e.g., "I'll hurt myself if you end our relationship."). According to some theorists-therapists (e.g., Laing, 1969), extortion within family relationships is quite common.

As mentioned, it appears that all criminal offenders use power in some form during the commission of their offenses. There would not, by definition, be an offense if, for example, an individual faced with a request for money immediately handed over all available cash – this could be a simple case of obliging generosity to a beggar's request rather than a grudging acquiescence to a robber's demands. Sexual offenders inevitably use at least one source of power, if not several, during the commission of an offense because, again, there would be no offense if there were true and complete consent on the part of a willing sexual partner. Many offenders I have encountered in my work rely very much on authority because they are fathers, priests, teachers, and psychologists. They are able via competence, personal love, reward, or punishment to compel victims to acquiesce to their demands. Choice of tactics to gain victim compliance is due to a number of factors including personal history/experience, social status, degree of social inequality, class and ethnicity, and this points to one problem with Wrong's (1979) analysis of power. According to Wrong, such factors are unimportant in the final analysis. If, however, a young male immigrant who is serving as a church altarboy is ordered by his priest to perform a sexual act, for example, how can a variety of social factors (e.g., immigration status, ethnicity, parental wealth) not enter into an analysis of the situation? The compliance in this example is due directly to the nature of the relationship and the characteristics of the victim.

As forensic clinicians, we often refer to a sex offender's "victim grooming", or the process, sometimes very lengthy, of preparing a target individual for sexual victimization. This process necessarily involves the use of power. Individuals who are selected as victims must be probed in terms of weak points. Weaknesses include the potential victim's likelihood of succumbing to persuasive arguments, vulnerabilities with respect to authority figures, and vulnerabilities that might provide a basis for extortion. A clear weak point with most children as potential victims concerns their lack of physical strength, although in a few cases an ability to obtain and to use a weapon might overcome any physical strength deficits. A single case of sexual abuse might involve a number of different sources of power. An offender might begin with gentle persuasion (e.g., "You really want to do this, don't you?"), switch to a threat of force when a victim is isolated (e.g., "If you don't take off your clothes, I'll hurt you."), and use extortion after the incident (e.g., "If you tell anyone, I'll say that you wanted it!").

Recognizing that sexual offenders employ power, however, does not answer the question of the role of power, and any consequent emotional "pay-off" (e.g., elation, self-satisfaction) or sense of confidence, in the causal structure of sexual assault. Is control a primary reason for sexual assault? Is sex a primary cause? The answer may be much more complex than many might think, or hope. PCT can potentially shed some more light on the reasons behind sexual assault and abuse.

Power and control in sexual assault

We have been told and reminded for quite some time (e.g., Quinsey, 1977, 1986) that we should not view sexual offenders – or even subtypes of offenders, such as those who prey exclusively on children – as a homogeneous group. There appear to be a number of significant differences among sub-types of sexual offenders. Work by many researchers, notably Prentky and Knight (e.g., 1991; Knight, Carter, and Prentky, 1989), has shown that there appear to be distinct subtypes of sexual offenders distinguishable on a num-ber of variables including, for lack of a better term, motivational factors. Empirically-based typologies by Prentky and colleagues, as well as work by other researchers, have shown, for example, that rapists can be divided into four or more distinct types. Consider a general typology of rapists as exploitative, compensatory, displaced anger, and sadistic.

Exploitative rapists, perhaps comprising a majority of men who assault adults sexually, tend to use power to achieve sexual gratification. They do not generally care about the harm they cause their victims because they are very self-absorbed. They know or care only about their own desires, and they will use any means possible to satisfy them, including using drugs or alcohol to incapacitate their intended victims. Most date rapists probably can be viewed as exploitative. Thus, while any and all types of power can and will be used by these offenders to gain victim compliance and overcome any resistance, their primary interest is their own sexual satisfaction. Power, therefore, is a means to an end rather than an end in itself.

Compensatory rapists, too, seem to be interested primarily in sexual con-quest. They tend to be socially inept individuals who believe that women need to be pressured into sexual activity and relationships. They may honestly believe myths surrounding rape (e.g., "Women like it rough.", " 'No' really means 'yes'."); nonetheless, they will use a variety of power bases in order to overcome resistance. They are often caught after their first or second assaults because of their naive views, and accompanying tendency to give out phone numbers or addresses in order to repeat the encounter. Compensatory rapists use power to compensate for social inadequacy, although only to the extent that they need to overcome resistance.

Displaced anger rapists are not interested in sex per se. They are keen on seeking revenge for perceived transgressions from an individual who seems to be a member of a particular group (e.g., ex-wives, feminists, domineering women) who caused the original pain. The anger, often long repressed or controlled, is expressed in the form of extreme violence in order to make the particular victim suffer as a result of her or his perceived inclusion in the offending group. Sexual violence or humiliation is only part of the attack and the wish to make the victim suffer as extensively as possible. The main intent, here, is not really sexual but the use of power to achieve an indirect form of revenge.

Sadistic rapists, even though they are often depicted in films and on tele-vision, are likely the least common. People who gain sexual pleasure from making others suffer are, at least in my clinical experience, rather few and far between. There is a confusion here between sex and violence, where violent assault has taken the place of normative sexual interests and activity (see Chapter 1). In a sense, sexual satisfaction is a goal of this rapist, but physical force and extreme pain and suffering on the part of the victim is the only way to achieve such release and expression.

Other examples – such as the distinction made between fixated or obsessed child molesters and regressed or situational molesters (Hollin and Howells, 1991) – exist throughout the literature on sexual offenders. Such typologies are useful in reducing the complexity of bizarre, disturbing, and perplexing behaviour. They may assist police investigators in apprehending a certain type of offender by highlighting general behavioural factors, and they may help potential victims or social action groups determine the most effective defense strategies when confronted by a particular type of offender. Ultimately, however, such typologies are limited for use by forensic clinicians because they discard so much useful individual information in order to force offenders into a limited number of categories. Again, returning to my original argument for more dimensionality to our consideration of sexual offenders, this loss of information is critical to any psychological assessor or psycho-therapist wanting to understand in a meaningful manner the underlying reasons for a particular assault or intended offense. Psychosocial details can provide insights into idiosyncratic beliefs or values that might provide a key to successful therapy. They can, in short, determine whether we have an efficacious intervention or experience a long and frustrating waste of valuable time. We need to take such details into consideration in light of a theory that considers how power impacts on a particular individual as offender and as victim of his own behaviour.

A number of studies and theories (e.g., Quinsey, 1986; Marshall and Barbaree, 1990) have emphasized the lack of social skill displayed by sex offenders, particularly those who molest children. This is undoubtedly the case if we view social skill narrowly as a set of behaviours (e.g., displaying respect, appropriate self-disclosure, politeness) that produce long-term, inti-mate relationships. Is not the brandishing of power, in whatever form, a form of social skill? Does not obtaining gratification from a relationship, however fleeting, in the face of resistance not demonstrate social skill? I think that it does, and I would suggest that many sexual offenders, far from being pathetic and ineffectual losers, are very skillful, not just in avoiding detection but in the use of various forms of power. I have long been amazed by certain clients, some working as priests and therapists but others who collect waste for a living, who are able to read people so flawlessly. In effect, they are able to assess personal constructs in an instant and exploit important ones. Based on their insights, they are able to employ the most careful manipulation, per-suasive arguments, and various forms of authoritative power in order to gain their victims' compliance. These are not crass, knife-waving goons or buf-foons but extremely clever individuals who, knowing what they want, have the skills to achieve it. In some cases, they are able to conceal their deeds involving many victims for many years. My point here is not to applaud the efforts of people who use and abuse others by employing subtle tactics, but we need to keep in mind that those who abuse others sexually have abilities and, in many cases, many redeeming features. Their skills, unfortunately, are obscured by their malevolence.

Recognition of the skills of many sex offenders is important for a number of reasons. First, and this point will be discussed in more detail in Chapter 5, we as clinicians need to build on existing strengths rather than pick away at personal deficits. A view of someone who has abused others sexually as lacking in any positive attributes, perhaps mirroring the manner in which they see themselves but more likely employing a "halo effect" in person perception, is not a realistic perspective and not likely to produce quick or even positive movement in therapy. Perhaps more importantly, villifying sexual offenders and creating extreme caricatures will only make a real abuser more difficult to spot. In fact, most individuals who offend sexually are not dishevelled, dwarfish men in dirty trenchcoats who lurk in bushes and live in abandoned automobiles; they are more likely to be well-dressed and respectable middle-class men who live in the suburban house next door. How often are we shocked by the news story about the successful family doctor who abused children in his surgery for years, or the venerated parish priest who abused many teenaged girls in the church hall? We should not be surprised at all, but all too often it is an unbelievable tale. No doubt this contributes to the ability of many abusers to fly below the community radar – the radar is either not working or is pointed in the wrong direction! Another consequence of what could be termed our "extreme deviant" stereotype of sexual abusers is that often the eccentric or "odd" individuals in our communities are the ones initially identified quickly as suspects in sexual assault cases: the man who is generally a loner but seems to relate well to children or the long-haired vagrant are often detained by the authorities. They have become our "usual suspects" because of our stereotypes of sex offenders. In a number of famous cases throughout Western countries, such as the Milgaard case in Canada (Karp and Rosner, 1991), these "oddballs" or deviants are convicted of horrendous sexual assaults or sex murders with little or no evidence. To put an end to such outrageous injustice, it is not enough to point fingers at the police and demand better training and more complete investigations. The police are like all of us – indeed, they are us – and operate with the same views and stereotypes.

Personal construct theory and the social world

Jahoda (1988), Burkitt (1996), and others have pointed out that personal construct theorists have not adequately considered the social world. In the language of PCT, social elements appear beyond the range of convenience of PCT. According to Jahoda, PCT has, at least until the late 1980s, had little concern for a real world inhabited by real social entities. To counter this position, Epting *et al.* (1996) and Leitner *et al.* (1996), among others, have argued that PCT has the potential for an account of the social that far exceeds contemporary theoretical contributions. While they may well be correct, to date this potential has not been realized. Many PCT-influenced contributors have attempted to address the social using PCT as a foundation in a variety of formulations. Notwithstanding the efforts of Bannister (1979), Duck (1973, 1979), Horley (1991), Procter and Parry (1978) and Stringer (1979), I do not believe that the social psychological aspects of PCT have been developed or expanded significantly. This is very much the case with respect to social power.

From a personal construct perspective, power has been defined by Rowe (1994) as "the ability to get other people to accept your definition of reality" (p. 29). Following Rowe, Leitner *et al.* (1996) described power as "the ability to influence another individual's construct system" (p. 323). On the surface, these similar views of power may appear adequate from a psychological perspective, but they fail to consider variations of power and power relations. In a very important respect, they miss the basic ways that power is wielded in everyday social interaction. Perhaps an occupational hazard for many psychologists, especially PCT-influenced psychologists, is mistaking thoughts rather than events as all important. All too often in contemporary psychology, real people and processes are obscured by psychological referents and processes. PCT, to account for social relations adequately and become a truly social psychological theory, needs to take very seriously a very basic component in the theory, elements, and nature of different types of elements. Specifically, there has been significant consideration of the nature of personal constructs but, with few exceptions (cf., Husain, 1983; Horley, 1988b), very little consideration of the nature of what constructs are applied to (i.e., elements). Kelly posited a real world populated with real people, but rarely does PCT accept and consider the attributes of elements, let alone the all too real attributes of elemental interstices. While there is a wide variety of possible elements, my concern here is with social elements (i.e., people, social groups) exclusively.

For someone trained in sociology and education, Kelly (1955) is strangely silent about the nature of social elements. Kelly does not offer any discussion about the characteristics of people or larger social entities except in the relative terms of the language of construction. Clearly the relativity of tallness versus shortness of people can be considered and debated, but there is little debate over a characteristic such as height. It can, and typically is captured using a metric or standard that defies debate except by the grossly ignorant, the floridly psychotic, or the painfully argumentative. Hair colour, annual income, ethnicity, and a wealth of other personal characteristics are the sum total of an individual's physical and biographical existence. While height and weight may be nonsensical characteristics when applied to larger social entities (e.g., nation states), there are corresponding characteristics that can be considered part of their composition. Population, gross domestic product, bordered land area, and similar indices are applied typically to national groupings. A variety of characteristics appear to apply to all social elements that are beyond consideration of relativistic constructions. While we could debate the appropriateness of any label or metric, the point is that some characteristics exist that apply to any social element.

One additional yet vital feature of all social elements regardless of social grouping level is power. Just as he was unconcerned with social class (Procter and Parry, 1978), Kelly (1955) was unconcerned with social power. Indeed, there appears to be an apparent connection, perhaps a necessary one, between class and power, but this point must be placed in parentheses for now. Actually, Kelly seemed to dismiss power as a relevant consideration, except in terms of construction, when he wrote that to "recognize that 'force' is a feature of many personal construct systems is, of course, not tantamount to embodying the notion of force in the psychology of personal constructs" (p. 240). Kelly, however, was referring to psychological attributes, or analytic units within psychology, as opposed to actual social attributes. To do otherwise would push PCT into the camp of idealism and compromise the constructivistic project that he presented so carefully.

Power, as a relational characteristic between all social elements, is very distinctive not only because it bridges the gulf of social grouping level (i.e., individual versus collective) but it appears to bridge the gap between social elements in a literal sense. Power defines the relationships among social elements. The conduct of people is very much determined by such aspects, and the determination does not just refer to the construal processes of the actors. While considerations about construct validation (see Epting et al., 1996; Leitner et al., 1996) are pertinent, they may have little to do with the nature of a social interaction. If two individuals meet on a street, with one producing a revolver and demanding fellatio from the second, the various constructions of the assault victim undoubtedly mean little to the gun-wielder so long as the behaviour (i.e., oral sex) is accomplished. All that can usefully be questioned in such a situation are the meanings of certain terms (e.g., "What's a 'blow job'?", "Does he mean right here and now in the street?"), the intent of the gun-wielding individual (e.g., "Is he prepared to pull the trigger if I refuse?"), and other similar considerations. While the gun qua power is in play, the relationship, however brief, is directed by the will of the gun's possessor. To pretend otherwise by an unarmed victim could lead to a sudden and violent death. In most everyday social interactions, another person's constructions are secondary, if relevant at all, to more primary considerations such as obtaining goods and services, whether through the use or the abuse of power.

Power, therefore, is a term applied to a relational characteristic that is real. If power were illusory in an ultimate sense as Rowe (1994) would have us accept, it would be silly to speak of powerful and powerless people, as she does. Perhaps the best that we could do is refer to "dupers" and "duped". While this falls far short of acceptable (e.g., it does not allow us to engage broader discussions within the social sciences on power), it does remind us of one aspect missing in many discussions of power. How do we account for voluntary acceptance of directions that are not in our own interest? Can we be duped, either individually or collectively? The answer is "Of course" and, according to some theorists, it happens quite regularly. The Marxist notion of "false consciousness" refers to the cognitive distortion involving social contradictions and the denial of class interests due to ideology from extended exposure to propaganda. False consciousness describes a situation where we can and do deny ideas and actions that are in our own interest in favour of ideas and actions that we accept but are actually in others' interests. Sartre (1956) presented a similar notion, "bad faith", or lying to oneself. Strictly speaking, bad faith refers to the paradoxical situation whereby, through a conscious and free choice, an individual denies his or her ability to make a free choice. More broadly, however, bad faith can be seen as the denial of beliefs and actions that are in one's own interest. Through propaganda and other sources, we can certainly, at times, be duped into accepting that which is harmful to our own interests and not resist others' attempts to get us to do their bidding.

Power exists in many forms, from the obvious use of gross physical force to the more subtle arts of persuasion and manipulation. While it may involve the ability to define reality, or to direct construct use and definition in PCT terms, power is not just "in the head" of construing individuals. We likely should ask, however, as good constructivists: Can power exist in the head as a construct? The answer appears to be a qualified "yes". Fransella and Adams (1966), for example, described the case of an arsonist who seemed to be interested in setting fires for the sense of power and control that came from the destruction of others' property. Consideration of this issue will allow us to to return to the original, unanswered question concerning the role of power in sexual assault.

Sex offenders and their victims: capitulation to powerlessness

Unquestionably, power can be viewed as a construct without diminishing its status as a relational component. This is akin to viewing any person, a social element in the language of PCT, as a construct (e.g., "Like mother–not like mother"), which does not compromise her or his ontological status as a real person. Powerful–powerless, predator–prey, wolf–sheep, master–slave, and boss–bitch are just a few of the power-relevant construct pairs that my clients have reported to me over the years. Generally, they view themselves on the more aggressive or dominant pole of the construct. As one client remarked recently, "Who in his right mind would want to be weak prey like sheep?" I do not, however, believe that sex offenders see themselves as all powerful and in charge of their destinies. Actually, the opposite appears true, at least initially. Many if not most sexual offenders are aware of an inherent vulnerability, a force within them that they are powerless in the face of, and they attempt to compensate for this powerlessness.

Frequently, sex offender clients of mine have described themselves as sex addicts. They crave sex constantly on their terms and the craving is continuous and all engrossing. If they are unable to gain satisfaction from a partner, and few can for long periods, they will turn to a prostitute or an unwilling man, woman, child, or, in a few cases, animal. Some are not very particular sexually while others are very choosy about a victim. This addiction metaphor has been expanded by some in the treatment field, and specialized therapy groups now exist for sex addicts. Although the focus of many of these groups are so-called "nymphomaniacs" and "Don Juans" – in other words, the sexually compulsive – some groups and clinicians encourage more serious sexual abusers to join. Setting aside concerns about the nature of the treatment, the conceptualization of deviant sexual behaviour as addiction is troublesome. As Peele (1995) and others have pointed out, the "treatment industry" has expanded the notion of addiction to include all forms of troublesome or habitually maladaptive behaviour and based it on a notion, addiction, that emphasizes weakness on the part of the sufferer. An addict has no willpower, no possibility of resisting the addictive substance or activity, at least not without constant involvement with a therapist or a therapeutic group. Peele (1997) has argued that, at least in the United States, such a development has advanced to a point that most U.S. citizens have at least one addiction that dominates and controls them. Due to this "diagnosis", or conceptualization, they are pouring billions of dollars into an industry that only feeds their sense of powerlessness. This may be less true for sex offenders, in part because there are few therapists interested in working with them on a full-time basis, but there is some comfort experienced by the offenders who do get involved. They feel relieved of any shame that they experienced as a result of their sex assaults because, after all, they were helpless to resist in the face of their addiction. The offenders I know who have become involved in a formal addiction view have become zealots, and generally attempt to convince fellow prison inmates, or anyone who will listen, about the benefits of joining one addiction group, or a specific addiction therapist, or another.

Most sexual offenders, even without participating in a formal movement or established group, come to recognize that they have an innate, congenital, or deep-seated problem that they find it impossible to resist. No doubt many are convinced of such a "condition" or "disorder" by clinicians, perhaps forensic clinicians, who, in the process of an assessment session, discuss a particular diagnosis. Others likely acquire the perspective from popular books, the media, friends, or family members. Whatever the source of understanding, it can often overwhelm them on first consideration. The quote at the beginning of this chapter was provided by a former high school teacher, a well-educated man who possessed graduate degrees, who scribbled a few notes for me (rather quickly I would add, and hence the poor grammar used in the quote) about his self-image. For him, the feeling of desire for his young students, for whom he claimed to have been concerned about deeply, was so powerful that he succombed to fondling and sex games with students and other youths. After being labelled a pedophile, he believed that there was no cure, especially after the various anti-androgen medications prescribed to curb his deviant sexual behaviours proved ineffective. He slipped slowly into despondency and, while not actively suicidal, had given up hope for change when we first met.

Many of the harsh and repulsive self-labels employed by some repeat sex offenders, such as those above (e.g., wolf, predator), seem to come after a period of hopelessness and resignation to "one's fate". They become, in a sense, a way of taking back control of one's self and life in that the offender, rather than being weak and helpless regarding his sexual compulsion, claims it as his own. He truly becomes a serious, long-term threat by accepting the various means by which he can see himself as in charge and dominant, the powerful one in the relationship with potential victims. He has truly accepted the role of sex offender or sexual predator at this point. Even the most vicious and sadistic sex killers I have met have admitted, usually only after I have earned their trust, that they really did not know what to make of themselves at first with respect to their harmful, abusive behaviour. They were uncomfortable about the attacks that they were planning, and the first victim, often not murdered or even badly injured physically, haunted them. At the same time, there was something that was compelling or deeply satisfying about the assault. It was only over time and usually following more violent experiences that they gained the sense that these offenses against others were indeed quite acceptable. They were doing what they were supposed to by actualizing their "true selves". The violence, at this point, had become an integral part of how they defined themselves. It had become, or was soon to become, truly a way of life (Winter, 2003b).

May (1972) has presented the interplay between power and powerlessness well. He sees a large portion of life dedicated to the conflict between powerfulness and powerlessness. While too much power may corrupt, too little power is equally if not more corrupting from May's perspective. More often than not, when we consider sexual offenders and their victims, we think of the victims as being powerless and being left even more powerless by their victimization (Berliner, 1991). Offenders, however, can feel powerless while stalking or assaulting victims. In a sense, the victims have power over the offenders, although only in a rather indirect and, ultimately, unsatisfactory manner. Part of the powerlessness of the offender may be due to previous victimization that he himself has endured. I have been asked on more than one occasion how an act that was reminiscent of a horrible childhood experience could be repeated. My answer generally is that the earlier experience left its mark psychologically, not just in terms of physical and emotional pain and turmoil but in the seed that was planted in the abused individual's own self-identity. Obviously, not all victims of sexual abuse go on to abuse others, but those who do might trace an altered sense of self to their own victimization. An assault during childhood or adolescence, when self-identity is malleable and open to change, can raise the possibility within the victim that not only are they somewhat responsible but may actually have enjoyed the abuse. Perverted, sick, screwed up, strange, conflicted, and confused are terms that I have been told by offenders applied to their own victimization. They began, as a function of their own experiences, to question who they must have been to allow such an experience to occur. Remarkably, some of those most confused were the ones least injured physically by the abuse. Because there was a positive aspect to the assault (e.g., attention from a valued adult, emotional support), they wondered who they must be to participate in this sort of encounter or relationship, and as a result they began to construe themselves as "different" in various specific ways.

It appears that sexual assault is not a simple result of the abuse of power; in fact, there does not appear to be a simple answer to the question, "Why do some individuals commit sexual assault?" If pressed, we could argue, consistent with my previous point, that sexual assault is all about self-validation. That argument, however, would be far too simplistic. If non-abusive sexual relationships, or even brief sexual encounters, are very diverse in terms of meanings for the participants, why should abusive ones be any simpler? While power might be a tool of abusers, and perhaps an extremely attractive one for some offenders, it appears to be a means to an end, and the end is not a singular one. Power, expressed in the form of constructs, appears extremely complex.

Power, expressed as a construct, appears likely to change over the course of time, and the time frame may be less than a "criminal career"; it may be a matter of weeks or even the course of a single assault. One of my clients, a thin university student in his early twenties, was arrested for a series of assaults on female students. They began, according to both police reports and my client, as a drunken party joke when, while relieving himself outside after far too much to drink, a woman stumbled upon him urinating. He reported that he did not even remember the episode clearly, but remembered that the feeling that came over him on discovery by the woman – he claimed not even to remember her reaction to him – was a very pleasant one. His next offense, within weeks of the first incident, involved the much more deliberate stalking of another woman. He followed her in his car until he had an opportunity to expose his genitalia. His final assault was his most violent and, again, it came only weeks after the second. He walked around his neighbourhood until he found an attractive woman who, after he exposed himself, kept walking past him. He ran after her, threw her to the ground, and forced her to touch his genitalia. He claimed to have no insight into his need for escalating violence, but he did volunteer that the hunt for a victim was like a drug that required more and more to get the same effect. Was power over his victims the drug that he needed? It could just as easily have been the sexual reassurance needed by a twenty-something virgin who seemed awkward around others, especially women. Unfortunately, I was privy to no further information because he gained early release from his sentence of mere months, no doubt due to his legal representation and his well-to-do parents, a fine example of a successful outcome due to the mobilization of power.

Power, as a relational characteristic, can no doubt colour or direct relationships in profound ways, but the idea that power is an end, as opposed to an enhancer, for sex offenders is not compelling. Power does, however, need to be considered as a factor in all sexual assaults, and any theory, such as PCT, that avoids consideration of the role of power in social relations, especially abusive ones, does so at its own peril. PCT need not ignore power, or regard it as "all in your head". Instead, an additional recognition of power as both a real, inter-elemental relational characteristic and the basis for some personal constructs only serves to strengthen the theory.

Chapter 4

Alternative approaches to the psychological assessment of sex offenders

Hope you know what's wrong with me, because I sure don't.
(A. D., incarcerated for multiple indecent acts in public,
personal communication)

According to Kelly (1955) and most PCT-oriented clinicians (see Winter, 1992a, 2003a), a basic premise of psychological assessment, indeed all clinical work, within PCT is a credulous approach to dealing with clients. For Kelly (1955), if you really want to know what a person is like, and what might be bothering them, all you need to do is ask directly because the individual may well be able to indicate, in some manner, what they are about and what they are experiencing. By adopting this credulous approach, the clinician "never discards information given by the client merely because it does not conform to what appear to be the facts" (Kelly, 1955, p. 322). Of course, some clients, and very likely most clients who have committed sexual offenses, have a vested interest in presenting a version of events that leads a clinician to incorrect inferences. Indeed, in some jurisdictions the interest may be a matter literally of life and death. Even falsehood contains some useful information, and Kelly would have all clinicians and assessors interested in complete and useful psychological inquiries take all information provided by a client seriously. According to Kelly (1955), a "perceptive clinician always respects the content of his client's 'lies,' although he is equally careful not to be misled by them" (p. 322). In the context of understanding violent offenders, especially murderers, Winter (2003b, 2007) has written extensively about the nature and role of Kelly's credulous approach. Winter (2007) has also discussed the limits of therapeutic credulity. This issue of credulity and the implications that it has for both assessment and psychotherapy is significant enough, and potentially misleading enough, to warrant further reference throughout the following two chapters.

As noted earlier, Kelly (1955, 1958a) had little use for traditional psychological or personality assessment techniques, neither objective nor projective techniques, because neither allowed an assessee to provide what he or she was actually thinking in any direct manner. His distaste for objectives, or standardized techniques (e.g., Minnesota Multiphasic Personality Inventory) used to examine a limited number of predetermined professional constructs like pathological personality traits, seems to have been exceeded by his disapproval of projectives, or devices (e.g., Thematic Apperception Test) intended to permit an assessee to project intention into somewhat ambiguous stimuli. In fact, he admitted that "projective testing may properly be considered a direct approach to personal constructs . . . [insofar as a]nything a person does can be interpreted as a projection of his personal constructs" (Kelly, 1955, p. 202). On the whole, however, Kelly appeared to mistrust all traditional assessment procedures, and he developed new techniques that fall beyond easy classification into existing categories.

Routine assessment of sexual offenders may include psychophysiological assessment such as penile plethysmography. Penile blood flow may provide useful data about sexual preferences for some offenders (Quinsey and Earls, 1990), but it is unlikely to reveal important information about the processes underlying deviant sexual behaviour for a majority of offenders (Marshall, 2006). Most sex offenders do not show deviant penile response profiles. While I must admit that I have and still would conduct or recommend such assessments for some sex offender clients, I also recognize a number of problems with penile plethysmography. The laboratory conditions and equipment necessary for proper assessments are very expensive, and the effort required for appropriate construction of such a facility is significant, not an undertaking to be assumed lightly. The cost and the difficulty of conducting such assessments may not be justified by the nature of the assessment results.

One overriding concern that I share with Marshall (2006) about the regular use of such assessment is the message provided indirectly to clients. Although unlikely intentional, the nature of penile plethysmography may deliver a clear understanding to an assessee that the source of the problem is between the legs rather than between the ears (i.e., genitalia are at fault rather than the construal processes that control the genitalia). Offenders routinely ask me after such an assessment about "equipment function" rather than any underlying reasons why their equipment might perform in any bizarre manner. In other words, mind is ignored in favour of bodily dysfunction. Sometimes the questions turn to biochemical levels or even neurotransmitter processes, but the discussions tend to be concentrated on somatic issues rather than psychosocial or emotional ones. For me, the roots of the problem almost always lie in the more ethereal parts of human functioning, the mind, which seems to be the most significant human "sexual organ". If conducted, and only for very good reasons (e.g., long history of very deviant acts), the explicit message delivered both before and after psychophysiological assessments of all types, especially penile plethysmographic ones, should be that the procedure is only used to reveal sexual responses that are based on underlying fantasies, thoughts, or feelings.

For all PCT-oriented clinicians, meanings are key in terms of understanding our clients' actions, including the deviant sexual behaviours of certain clients. The assessment of meaning is not necessarily quick or easy, but well worth the effort. Some formal assessments for examining meaning have been discussed in the previous chapter, and some will be presented in more detail here. Clearly, however, simple interview questions can access personal meanings, and these may represent the most straightforward points of access to meaning. A question like "What do you mean by that?" can be the most effective and direct means of allowing a client to elaborate on an important construct that he uses to order or to understand his experience. Asking the questions, and listening carefully to the answers, can yield extremely useful information about the origins and maintenance of deviant sexual behaviours. A proper initial interview with a sex offender client is important not only to collect useful information but also to provide the basis for the proper therapeutic relationship. If a client is convinced that he is being heard and understood, trust can follow readily. Conversely, if a client is given the impression that no matter what he says he will simply be ignored or perceived as "just another child molester", trust will be difficult to establish at any point in the therapeutic relationship. When formal assessment procedures, such as the ones that follow in this chapter, are employed, they must not be conducted in a mechanical fashion. Any technique, however sophisticated or valid, can be rendered invalid and pointless by a ham-handed test administrator. If presented as a tool for structuring and assisting a client in presenting his story or his truth – really, his meaning in terms of his problematic behaviour – the technique can be a valuable device for furthering the collection of important information. Psychological assessment should be viewed as the process by which valid psychological predicates are applied to people and, while we as assessors have an important role to play in the interpretation of the information provided by a client, we should not compromise the assessment process by mechanical or uncaring administration of any formal assessment techniques. This said, not all techniques are created equal, and some of the more important for my work with sexual offenders will be discussed now.

Techniques for personal construct assessment

The repertory test

Kelly's (1955) repertory test (rep test) is a broad-ranging assessment approach to the elicitation and examination of an individual's vast array, his or her repertoire, of personal constructs. The rep test comes in a variety of formats, including card sorts (e.g., Badesha and Horley, 2000) and a verbally administered group format (Kelly, 1955), but the most popular format by far is the repertory grid technique (rep grid). The rep grid (see Fransella *et al.*, 2004) is the rep test in matrix form. The rep grid has played an integral role as both a research instrument and a clinical tool in the development of personal construct theory. Indeed, some form of repertory grid procedure has been used in over 90 per cent of published empirical research in personal construct theory (Neimeyer *et al.*, 1990). This methodology also has been employed widely by researchers outside the field of personal construct psychology (Adams-Webber, 1989).

The rep grid is essentially a complex sorting task in which a list of elements is categorized dichotomously in terms of each of a set of bipolar dimensions (see Figure 4.1). An assessor can either elicit a sample of personal constructs from each respondent individually, or simply supply the same "standard" set of dimensions to all subjects alike. The data elicited from each respondent are entered into a separate two-dimensional matrix or grid in which there is a column for every element and a row for every construct. Each row–column intersect in this grid contains a symbol (e.g., a binary digit) indicating which pole of a given construct was applied to a particular element. Many forms of rep grid in current use, unlike Kelly's original procedure, require rating the elements on n-point scales where n is greater than 2. For example, 1 might represent the assignment of an element to (say) the left-hand pole of a construct, and n its assignment to the right-hand pole. Scalars within the range $2 \rightarrow n\text{-}1$ can be used to represent intermediate response alternatives. To permit a natural midpoint, n is usually a small odd number, such as 3, 5, or 7. As shown by Gaines and Shaw (1980), each pole of a given construct can be viewed as representing a predicate that designates a set, with or without distinct logical boundaries, and every rating as indicating a particular element's degree of membership in that set.

Kelly (1955) assumed that all constructs are bipolar in form, or have a binary format. Every construct represents a single dichotomous distinction (e.g., serious versus frivolous). Kelly defined the relationship between the alternative poles of each construct in terms of bipolar opposition or contrariety (see Husain, 1983). Repertory grid research utilizes this assumption sometimes without sufficient concern regarding the contrast pole that is often assumed rather than elicited. Kelly (1955) himself devised several different ways in which personal constructs can be elicited. His "difference method" is the single most commonly used of these approaches. In this method, respondents are presented with sets of three elements, or triads, and asked to indicate how two of them are alike in some important way in which they differ from the third (e.g., "My father and I are both tough while my sister is weak."). There is no strict requirement that the contrasts are genuinely bipolar. Mair (1967) observed that "the contrasts between poles of constructs often differ considerably from those that seem to be dictated by the logic of public language . . . studies seem to demonstrate enough variety in pole contrasts to encourage more attention to this problem in psychological measurement generally and grid measurement in particular" (p. 226). As Fransella and Bannister (1977) noted: "We may assume that

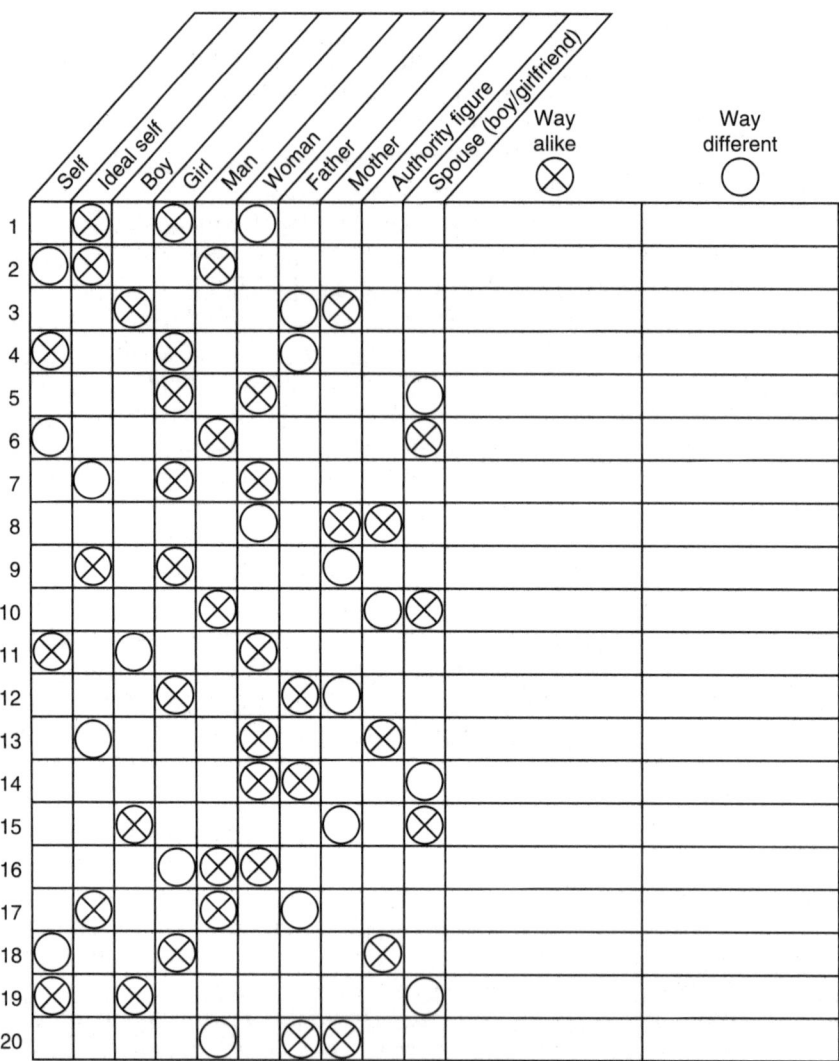

Figure 4.1 An example of the role construct repertory grid.

charitable to you means the same as charitable to me. But for you the opposite pole might be intolerant and for me hold strong opinions" (p. 105). Mair
(1967) found sufficient variety when respondents were asked to provide
contrast poles to provided constructs to warrant more explicit attention to
contrast constructs, particularly in view of the small but consistent effect
of overlapping endorsement of "opposite" constructs when construing the
same elements. He cautioned against our making inferences about construct
relationships regarding the implicit contrast pole and suggested that people

often use amalgamations of ideas rather than single verbal labels to describe others.

Epting *et al.* (1971) found that the "opposite method" (i.e., giving the opposite of the construct) elicited significantly more genuinely bipolar constructs. However, it also generated significantly less differentiated personal constructs; a finding subsequently replicated by Hagans *et al.* (2000) and Neimeyer *et al.* (2002). Hagans *et al.* (2000) suggested that there are two distinct ways in which the difference and the opposite methods might influence the kind of constructs which are elicited. First, instructions to provide the opposite of a given pole might elicit a more extreme contrast. For example, asking an individual to specify the opposite of "friendly" might elicit "hostile" rather than a less extreme response such as "aloof". In short, the opposite method creates a demand characteristic for more strongly valenced contrast poles. Second, the opposite method also allows the possibility that the contrast pole may not apply to any element in the grid. In contrast, the difference method requires that at least one element in the triad can be assigned to the contrast pole because it is elicited on the basis of that element's difference from the first two. The opposite method does not impose this specific constraint.

Hagans *et al.* (2000) pointed out that "differences between the opposite and difference methods of construct elicitation carry direct implications for measures of construct system structure" (p. 158). Elicitation instructions that require the distribution of ratings across both poles of constructs, as in the difference method, can increase differentiation between constructs. Methods that limit this distribution, or even allow all elements to be allotted to the same pole of a construct, can reduce overall construct differentiation. A pair of experiments by Hagans *et al.* (2000) showed that the opposite method elicited more extreme and negative contrast poles. They also observed that the negativity of contrast poles was correlated inversely with differentiation between constructs (i.e., constructs with more extreme and negative contrast poles were less differentiated). Moreover, when the influence of negativity per se was partialled out, there was no effect in terms of differentiation. These results support the hypothesis that the opposite method leads to the elicitation of more extreme contrasts that are then applied to a narrower range elements. Briefly, differences in the complexity, negativity, and bipolarity of personal construct systems are related to variation in the method of construct elicitation.

Relatively little research in personal construct theory has been concerned with evaluating repertory grid methodology in terms of its reliability and validity despite calls for more attention from some investigators (e.g., Chambers, 1985). An important study that examined the reliability and validity of a variety of repertory grid indices by Bavelas *et al.* (1976) produced some challenging results. They found, as did Adams-Webber (1970a), satisfactory agreement among different repertory grid measures assessing the same formal index (e.g., cognitive complexity, identification, construct constellatoriness), but they also found other indices unreliable over short time intervals such as one, two and three weeks. They argued that this lack of reliability at the structural level implied a lack of reliability at the content level as well, although this has not been found to be the case by other investigators (e.g., Sperlinger, 1976; Horley and Quinsey, 1995; Horley, 1996). Both Sperlinger (1976) and Horley (1996) reported moderate reliability in content areas, albeit with limited samples. Other explanations for Bavelas *et al.*'s findings are possible; for example, they themselves suggested that, first, not all the figures on the grid were within the range of convenience of all the constructs leading to some random responding and, second, the size of the grid (19 × 19) possibly produced random responding due to fatigue and impermeability. The questions raised by this study have been passed over too often in rep grid research. Some early research into grid methodology, while stressing its flexibility, tended to discount the importance of reliability. For example, Bannister and Mair (1968) took the position that "since there is no such thing as the grid, there can be no such thing as the reliability of the grid" (p. 156). It follows that questions concerning reliability and validity apply directly to the particular composite indices and methods of analysis employed rather than to repertory grid technique as a general measurement format.

In recent years, there has been a tremendous proliferation of new forms of the rep grid. Despite early warnings by Bonarius (1965) and others, clinicians have forged ahead with the development of novel and complex grid measures, often without much regard for reliability. Hagans *et al.* (2000) noted that "variations in grid methods affect not only the structure of the construct system, but also the nature of the constructs elicited" (p. 170). Continued use of the grid in PCT research requires a conscientious effort to investigate the strengths and limitations of the rep grid both in terms of structure and content. There does exist, however, some fairly convincing evidence that, whatever its limitations, repertory grid technique can be used to produce highly reliable measurements, some of which also provide strong support for its construct validity in terms of the central assumptions of PCT.

The degree of differentiation between self and others provides a good example of grid consistency. This factor can be defined in grid terms simply as the extent to which people assign themselves and others to the same poles of a set of dichotomous constructs (e.g., good vs. bad). It has been referred to in the relevant literature by a variety of different names, including "identification" (Jones, 1961), and "assimilative projection" (Bieri, 1955). Reported estimates of the temporal or test–retest reliability of this composite index have ranged from 0.86 to 0.95 (Pedersen, 1958; Jones, 1961; Benjafield and Adams-Webber, 1975; Sperlinger, 1976; Feixas *et al.*, 1992). There is also evidence that some of its component substructures, for instance, the degree of differentiation between mother and self, are highly reliable (Pedersen, 1958).

Indeed, self-differentiation may be one of the most stable of rep grid indices (Winter, 1992a). Moreover, observed correlations between this particular measure and several other formal indices of rep grid structure tend to be higher than their own test–retest correlations. These include the overall degree of statistical association between constructs, the average distance between figures, the number of significant linkages between constructs, and the explanatory power of the first factor (see Adams-Webber, 1979, 1989). Thus, self-differentiation is not only both consistent and stable as a grid measure, but it also helps to explain much of the systematic variation in other aspects of grid structure. It is possible that this index represents an important factor in the organization of personal construct systems.

With respect to self–other differentiation in PCT research, Bannister and Agnew (1977), among other investigators, have hypothesized that, as children mature and gain in interpersonal experience, they should manifest gradual increases in the degree to which they differentiate between themselves and other persons. On the basis of this hypothesis, it can be predicted specifically that the extent to which children and adolescents distinguish between themselves and others on bipolar constructs will gradually increase throughout childhood and adolescence. In support of this hypothesis, Carr and Townes (1975) reported systematic increases in differentiation between self and others during late adolescence and early adulthood.

Strachan and Jones (1982) hypothesized that the degree to which adolescents differentiate themselves specifically from their parents also increases with age. As Winter (1992a) pointed out, a "particular aspect of identification with parents which has received some research attention is the extent to which an individual's identification with the parent of the same sex as himself or herself is greater than that with the opposite-sex parent" (p. 134). An early study by Giles and Rychlak (1965) indicated that students tend to characterize themselves as more similar to the parent of the same gender than to the parent of the opposite gender, although the results of Ryle and Breen (1972) suggest that this difference may hold only for women. In their guidelines to interpretation of rep grid data, Landfield and Epting (1987) recommended that we "observe whether mother is differentiated from father" (p. 132). Adams-Webber and Neff (1996) found a significant correlation between age and the degree to which children and adolescents between 8 and 18 differentiated themselves from parents of their own and opposite gender. Moreover, the extent of differentiation between the parents was correlated with the degree of differentiation of self from each parent. Across all 11 age groups, both boys and girls differentiated themselves more from parents of the opposite gender than from parents of the same gender. Although girls and boys differentiated themselves from their mothers to about the same extent, girls differentiated themselves from their fathers significantly more than did boys. It also has been found consistently that, when people evaluate themselves negatively on any bipolar construct, either elicited or supplied, approximately

50 per cent of other persons also will be evaluated negatively on that particular construct (Benjafield and Adams-Webber, 1975; Adams-Webber and Davidson, 1979; Adams-Webber and Rodney, 1983; Adams-Webber, 1989). Thus, "positive–negative asymmetry", which seems so ubiquitous in social cognition (see Warr, 1971), is specific to constructs in terms of which self is assigned to positive poles.

Depressed psychiatric patients, compared to various other groups, not only assign both themselves and others to the negative poles of more constructs, but they also characterize others as less similar to themselves (Space and Cromwell, 1980; Space et al., 1983). Space and Cromwell (1980) refer to this latter result as an unexpected finding, on the basis of which they suggest that "low identification with others should be included along with other features of depression" (p. 156). When Adams-Webber and Rodney (1983) instructed undergraduates to role play a negative mood following imagined experiences involving intense disappointment, there was a significant decrease in the proportion of similar-to-self evaluations. When the same participants enacted euphoric moods associated with imagined successes (in counterbalanced order), the proportion of "similar-to-self" judgments increased significantly. In a replication of this study by Lefebvre et al. (1986), the relative frequency of "similar-to-self" evaluations also decreased during the enactment of a "negative" mood and increased during the enactment of a "positive" mood.

The studies mentioned above are a healthy sign in the development of PCT methodology in that there is active interest and research into methodological issues raised by proliferating grid studies. The rep grid, however, is not the only technique available for PCT research. This is not readily apparent from the literature where the grid-based research dominates, sometimes with perfunctory references to its PCT underpinnings (Neimeyer, 1985). There is need in future research for a closer linking of theory and methodology, but there is a greater need for more creative exploration of alternative methodologies.

Various techniques consistent with PCT

Kelly (1955) provided more than one technique for assessing personality, although the wide use of the rep grid has overshadowed this fact. Self-characterization technique was suggested (Kelly, 1955) as an assessment consistent with PCT's credulous approach by asking a client directly about himself or herself. Self-characterization, similar to asking a client/assessee "Who are you?", involves a character sketch provided in the third person from the assessee. By describing himself or herself in an autobiographical yet somewhat distant manner, the individual may provide important information about salient personal constructs and their characteristic manner of anticipating events. Self-characterization technique appears to have been used infrequently, and typically in a clinical context (see Landfield and Epting, 1987; Winter, 1992a). It remains, however, a technique that can yield interesting data for personality investigators because of its appealing "open" format and ability to provide access to core constructs (Horley, 2005b). Horley and Johnson (2008) have discussed a treatment group for domestic abusers where self-characterization provided not only one approach to construct assessment but the framework for initial group discussions as members described their current selves.

Another interesting modification of the standard repertory grid has been introduced by Ryle and Lunghi (1970). Instead of using figures as elements they used relationships between people (e.g., John to Mary, Mary to John). Their dyad grid provides a measure of a person's perception of interpersonal relationships. Ryle and Lunghi favoured a repertory grid method because data are collected directly from the respondent so that the therapist's own theoretical constructs cannot bias it, and because the particular aims of therapy can be defined in grid terms and measured afterward. The dyad grid is analyzed in terms of two principal components (Slater, 1969) which can be diagrammed as orthogonal axes. Elements can be displayed on the diagram to illustrate the way in which relationships are construed (e.g., if the dyad lines for two elements are parallel, a similarity of reciprocal roles is suggested). The grid elucidates the way the respondent perceives a range of dyadic relationships such as Self–Mother, Self–Spouse, and Mother–Father. The dyad grid was recommended for investigating certain therapy clients for whom relationships are disturbed. It has also been used like the standard grid to assess the therapist's understanding of his or her client (Ryle and Lunghi, 1971). Ryle and Breen (1972) used the dyad grid to measure empathy in adjusted and maladjusted couples.

The grid technique has been expanded for exploring more specialized interests. Hinkle (1965) was interested in the implicative network of constructs in understanding the explanatory power of individual constructs. He wanted to examine the superordinate and subordinate relationships among constructs and in order to reveal this hierarchical structure he devised the implication grid or imp grid. The imp grid involves fairly elaborate means of deriving a construct hierarchy by a process called laddering. A person is asked why a particular pole of a construct is preferred and as a new construct is generated in explanation the question is repeated until no further dimensions are given. The implications of these constructs are then derived by having the person imagine himself or herself changing poles on a construct and then stating what other changes would occur as a result of the initial change. The imp grid is one of the few examples of grid modifications built upon sound theoretical bases, and it has been adapted by other investigators (e.g., Honikman, 1973). Honikman noted that gaining experience in a particular domain of activity fosters the development of implications among constructs that are specifically applied to events in that domain, and the more implications a particular construct carries throughout an individual's system the greater its subjective importance and immediate accessibility, as well as the lower likelihood that the individual will change a self-evaluation on the basis of the construct.

Our attempts (e.g., Horley and Quinsey, 1994, 1995; Horley *et al.*, 1997) to develop a technique to examine child molesters' thoughts about themselves and others based on the Osgood *et al.* (1957) semantic differential appear consistent with PCT assessment. Although the particular technique developed originally has been modified, and may require further modification (see Marshall *et al.*, 2003) to be very useful, the use of the semantic differential is one technique or, like the rep grid, a methodological approach that could be used to develop further forms of specific sex offender assessments. It has certain clear advantages (e.g., flexibility, less transparency) than some existing techniques in use for assessing offenders' constructs and cognitions (see previous chapter for examples). A somewhat related technique, the Implicit Association Test (IAT), was recently adapted for use with child molesters by a number of researchers (e.g., Gray *et al.*, 2005; Nunes *et al.*, 2007). The IAT is an indirect technique, administered via computer, that calculates the response latency between various bipolar terms (e.g., pleasant–unpleasant) and target terms (e.g., child, adult). Gray *et al.* (2005) showed that men convicted of sexual offenses against children revealed less response latency between children and sex than adults and sex, while Nunes *et al.* (2007) found a relationship between molesters' responses to children and attraction. Both concluded that the IAT could be a useful assessment of child molesters' thoughts about children and adults, and it is not difficult to see how the approach could be used with other sexual offenders (e.g., men who assault adults, those who exhibit genitalia in public) as well.

Personal projects matrix

Little (1987) argued convincingly that concern with purposive activity is or should be the focus of many areas within psychology. Rather than rely on existing units that appeared to capture activity, Little (1983) introduced a new unit of analysis, the personal project. The personal project is an interrelated sequence of actions intended to attain or maintain a state of affairs foreseen by an individual. A project can be an activity as limited as "Brushing my teeth" to as grand as "Finding a cure for cancer", with the level of phraseology likely betraying something significant about the person engaged in the activity (Little, 1983). For Little (1983, 1987), the examination of personal projects necessarily involves ecologically valid assessment in that social and physical environmental contexts of activity are accounted for.

Personal projects have been elicited and examined using a number of techniques, but most notably the personal project matrix (PPM) has been used (see Little, 1983; Palys and Little, 1983). The PPM is a matrix or grid technique that can be seen as one manifestation of Kelly's rep grid (Horley, 1988b) and, like the rep grid, it is based on Kelly's credulous approach to assessment (Little and Grant, 2006). In contrast to Palys and Little (1983), I (Horley, 1988b) argued that project dimensions – one set of analytic dimensions used by PPM respondents to examine their own personal projects – are not fundamentally different from Kelly's personal constructs. If personal constructs can be understood in terms of values and beliefs (Horley, 1991), so too can project dimensions, albeit with some care when provided dimensions or constructs are used. Thus, according to Horley (1987, 1988b), the choice of analytic units like personal constructs and personal projects are not an "either–or" situation, rather more of a "both–and" possibility. Constructs and projects appear to fit together, although it has to be admitted that personality traits and projects can be employed together too (Little, 2006).

The PPM, whether employed with constructs or used with trait measures, remains unexamined psychometrically. Certainly there are no results in terms of its use in forensic settings. The PPM has also been the basis of some non-forensic work on lifestyles (Horley et al., 1988; Horley, 1992). Walters (e.g., 1990, 2000) has argued that the concept of lifestyle is not only key to understanding the maintenance and change of criminal behaviour, but also is an important building block in an overarching theory in psychology. It is possible that the PPM could be a useful measure of criminal lifestyles, but this research has yet to be conducted.

One issue concerning the personal projects approach involves the question: "Is there a criminal project?" This question can probably be answered in any number of ways. On a simple level, there are likely many criminal projects from "Robbing the local convenience shop" to "Getting what I want from that good-looking girl". As assessors or therapists, we are unlikely to have access to any of them. Indeed, we may not want access to any of them given our duty to protect members of the community and the need to report specific threats. On another level, however, there may be many criminal projects that begin as any other activity, perhaps as well-intended attempts at self-improvement. "Staying away from drugs" or "Avoiding inappropriate sexual affairs" might be laudable attempts to avoid intrapersonal and interpersonal conflicts but, for some, the outcomes might be far more problematic than for other individuals. It could be suggested, too, that some projects are miscast from the start because they are staged in socially and physically impoverished environments that do not permit any likelihood of a successful completion. To what extent continued frustration at "Find a decent job" leads invariably to desperate and possibly criminal projects like "Get some cash by any means" is an open question.

Risk assessment

Determination of the risk posed by sexual offenders either on probation or released from custody has become an important consideration and activity among forensic mental health professionals (Craissati, 2004). Over the past several years, a number of techniques, such as the Sex Offender Risk Appraisal Guide (SORAG; Quinsey *et al.*, 1998), have been developed and tested extensively. In general, these techniques have performed reasonably well (e.g., Hanson and Thornton, 2000; Barbaree *et al.*, 2001). They do, however, possess limitations.

Most of the current crop of risk assessment devices, like the SORAG, rely on static demographic or background variables. To the extent that past behaviour predicts future behaviour, and it does do a reasonably good job for most of us, the strategy of employing mostly "tombstone" variables is a sound one. People do not behave in a completely consistent manner, however. Indeed, sometimes we change course rather radically after, perhaps, a significant lack of success either in a particular pursuit or life in general. Change, after all, is what psychotherapy is concerned with, and experiences with clients who do not make significant changes, especially improvements, during therapy are deemed failures. Dynamic risk predictors are in short supply in risk assessments (see Hanson and Thornton, 2000). The few dynamic items that do make it into present risk questionnaires are of dubious value. The SORAG, for example, does account for deviant sexual responses in the form of penile plethysmographic results but, as Marshall (2006) and others have noted, such data have little relevance to a majority of sexual offenders who reveal no deviant penile preferences. Overall, the amount of variance accounted for by risk assessments is moderate at best.

How can current risk assessment be improved? One problem appears to be the way that such assessments are conducted currently – they have become far too mechanical. It is not sufficient to sit down with a target individual in a prison interview room for ten minutes or, worse still, sit down with an individual's prison file for ten minutes. My intention in raising this issue is not to revisit the old issue of clinical versus actuarial prediction (Meehl, 1954), but to make the point that, ultimately, predicting risk is about knowing and understanding another individual. Only by taking the time and really getting to know and understand deeply one's clients, whether as a forensic clinician or a probation/parole officer, can one truly predict future harm, and a risk device, even a good one, is likely only a first step. When one of my clients astounds me with some unanticipated act of violence, aimed at himself or those around him, is it his responsibility for being inscrutable, or mine for not paying attention to what he was trying to tell me? Often, as clinicians, we are not paying attention to the messages our clients are giving us, perhaps because the messages are non-verbal and very subtle but perhaps because we are not really paying attention. Some of the blame for our lack of attention may be due to the conditions that many work under (e.g., extreme case loads, too many demands on time/attention from associates) but I think that part of the problem is due simply to our own professional distractions in terms of trying to construe clients in professional terms and categories that do not apply. Spending interview time thinking about the homosexual pedophile in the room is not only a time-wasting exercise but one that is distracting from the real information available from the client. What is being said or done by an individual client is central to understanding the individual and predicting his next move. I do not think enough forensic clinicians, and I would include myself here at times, are paying attention to what their clients are trying to tell them. True understanding of another is at the basis of risk assessment and practice. The issue of practice, beyond further effective treatment (see next chapter), is an important issue, and well beyond the scope of this book, but the interested reader is referred to a recent book by Craissati (2004).

Chapter 5

Psychotherapy with sexual offenders

> I see myself as a loser alot of the time, and a quitter ... I see myself a wreck that has to be fixed or scrapped ... I am fucked-up.
>
> (D. P., incarcerated for the sexual assault of a woman, personal communication)

Traditional psychotherapy with sexual offenders has included a wide range of very different approaches. These interventions vary from medical treatments such as anti-androgen medication (see Bradford, 1990) to strict behavioural techniques such as contingency management (see Laws and Marshall, 1990). The choices in treatment approaches have increased significantly over the past decade or two (see Cordess and Cox, 1996; Mobley, 1999). This expansion followed a period of pessimistic "nothing works" (Martinson, 1974) in offender rehabilitation, especially within North America.

A number of treatments assumed under the generic title of "cognitive-behavioural" appear effective (Andrews *et al.*, 1990; Gendreau, 1996), although some reviewers (e.g., Furby *et al.*, 1989) are far less positive about the efficacy of current approaches with sexual offenders. Following a brief overview of previous work in personal construct psychotherapy in general, this chapter will outline some of the approaches to psychotherapy compatible with PCT that I have used with sexual offenders. Some of these psychotherapies, such as fixed-role therapy (FRT), were developed by Kelly (1955) or later personal construct therapists, while others were developed by various therapists but appear consistent with the tenets of PCT. Problems encountered while delivering these therapeutic services to offenders will be discussed briefly, and cases will be presented to illustrate some forensic problems.

Brief review of the PCT treatment literature

PCT has been elaborated within the clinical context in terms of various forms of psychotherapy, with the rep grid and other PCT techniques used as adjuncts to clinical work. Most notable among the various books on psychotherapy and clinical work are Landfield (1971), Epting (1984), Landfield and Epting (1987), Winter (1992a), and Winter and Viney (2005). Landfield (1971) synthesized his work on therapeutic uses of PCT and elaborated grid techniques to be used in assessing both the content and structure of personal constructs. Landfield (1970, 1971) recommended assessing both because content indicates an individual's preoccupation while structure indicates how an individual's constructs are related. In his system, content can be analyzed into 22 categories representing a variety of meaning implications (e.g., social interaction, forcefulness, emotional arousal). Organization is measured in terms of the number of functionally independent constructions (FIC) or separate dimensions used by the subject. A low FIC score means that the constructs are highly integrated and organized while a high FIC score indicates that constructs are used independently of one another. Landfield (1970) found that patients who prematurely terminate therapy are less congruent with the therapist in the content of their construct systems than are clients who do not end therapy. He added that some client–therapist incongruency in conceptual structure is related to improvement in long-term cases. His approach to construct content analysis has been employed by a number of investigators concerned with grid content reliability (e.g., Horley, 1996) and the nature of construct content among client groups (e.g., Horley and Quinsey, 1995).

Using the self-ideal self discrepancy as the criterion measure for success in psychotherapy, Varble and Landfield (1969) found that the discrepancy decreased significantly from pre-therapy to post-therapy. The rep test enables measurement of the self concept and ideal self concept in terms meaningful to the individual by placing a patient's elicited dimensions on cards which are rank ordered from most to least important in understanding people, with the lowest and highest ranks defined as peripheral and core constructs respectively. Varble and Landfield found some support for Kelly's assertion that peripheral constructs change more quickly and easily than core constructs. Independent judges assessed improvement in the patients and the unimproved patients were found to have greater discrepancy scores. Changes in the self were more frequent than changes in the ideal.

Landfield (1976) offered a personal construct interpretation of suicidal behaviour. Suicide is seen within the framework of personal anticipation as failure to encompass or interpret relative social events. When a person's organization fails to minimize conflict, it constricts its focus until suicide may occur. The rep grid provides a measure of this constriction in two ways. The content may be constricted if the constructs are highly concrete, and the total number of ratings on the grid measures constriction in application of constructs. The FIC score measures disorganization. If the person's construct system is disorganized and constricted, the resulting failure to predict can result in dread of a total breakdown of any structure for comprehending life. Landfield found that a group of students who had failed in serious suicide attempts had significantly higher constriction scores than comparable students who were undergoing therapy but who were not suicidal. Grids were available for a number of the most suicidal in the sample before the attempt took place, thereby avoiding the usual problem in related research (i.e., data are collected only after the fact, rendering the state of mind of the potential suicide unknown).

Ryle and his colleagues have analysed rep grids in order to study therapeutic groups. Ryle and Lunghi (1969) recommended the use of the rep grid to provide an objective measure of variables of interest to the therapist. The therapist can examine the dispersion of significant people within a client's construct system and the aims of treatment can be translated into prediction of change in construct relationships. This provides a subtle and effective means of evaluating psychiatric treatment. Ryle and Lunghi (1970) modified the grid using relationships as elements, creating what they termed a "dyad grid", because they felt the rep grid method provided a means of collecting data directly from the patient without the bias of a therapist's own theoretical constructs. In addition, the aims of therapy could be defined in grid terms and measured afterward. The dyad grid is analyzed in terms of two principal components using Slater's INGRID program (Slater, 1969) which can be diagrammed as orthogonal axes. Elements can be displayed on the diagram to illustrate the way in which relationships are construed when the client's hopes and therapist's aims are relatively independent. Symptom loss and dynamic change, as indicated by the grid, were highly correlated.

The case of the grid is often extended beyond the single client to the group situation. Watson (1970b) used group members as grid elements, with constructs provided by the therapists. The constructs were thought to be important in understanding group activities (e.g., comparative constructs, "like me", or emotional constructs, "angry"). Each member was rated on a scale from 0–100 on each construct. These grids were used to provide hypotheses about the group, indicate therapeutic change, and reveal individual construct relationships. Watson (1972) found measurable changes during treatment, particularly among the patients, as opposed to the therapists, when the grids were completed at two three-month intervals. An empathy score was derived from the relationship between the subject prediction of ranking and the actual ranking by every other subject. As might be expected, certainly as one would hope, the therapist who was ranked highest on understanding, by the clients and by himself, had the highest grid score on empathy. There was a high correlation between grid empathy and rated empathy. The amount of overlap between own and others' constructs, shared experience, correlated highly with empathy, although patients high on understanding were able to depart from their own views in order to predict the view of others.

Rep grids have also been used as indicators of change in therapy situations (see Winter, 1992b), including forensic settings. Shorts (1985) employed a rep grid as a measure of change in personality and, more specifically, construing in individual therapy with a rapist. The alteration of self and other views on the part of this hospitalized client were interpreted by Shorts as evidence of the sensitivity and utility of the rep grid in therapeutic settings. Houston and Adshead (1993) also employed a rep grid as a measure of change for a small group of child molesters who participated in a community-based treatment group. Although a pilot project, Houston and Adshead found that change in grid results mirrored qualitative measures of change provided by the group leaders. They recommended that grids be used more often by therapists interested in more sensitive and less transparent change indices.

Research into the efficacy of PCT-based psychotherapy for offenders has been relatively limited and, like the situation in personal construct psychotherapy more generally (see Winter, 2003a), often based on case studies. Some of the forensic case studies reported in the clinical literature to date are difficult to interpret in terms of therapeutic result. Skene's (1973) report of the treatment using FRT of a "homosexual" is a good case in point. From Skene's description of the client, it is impossible to know whether the teenager being treated was sexually aggressive with young males at least five years his junior – hence, hebephilic to use current, psychiatric terminology – or was simply engaged in consenting sexual relationships with similar aged peers. Shorts' (1985) report of PCT psychotherapy with an adult male who assaulted adult females is rather unclear as to the result of therapy insofar as identifying with rapists at the termination of treatment is not necessarily the mark of success that many clinicians would accept. Case studies do suggest that various PCT-based treatments, especially FRT, can and have been used with some efficacy with arsonists (Fransella and Adams, 1966; Landfield, 1971), exhibitionists (Landfield and Epting, 1987; Horley, 1995), complex sexual deviations (e.g., Horley, 2005a), and mentally disordered offenders (Houston, 2003).

While there are few formal and systematic evaluations of psychotherapeutic programs, there is reason to believe that this situation is changing. Among the more formal evaluations of PCT-based offender therapies, Cummins (2003) has described a program that he offers for those with anger problems. Anger, although not necessarily a forensic issue per se, can clearly lead to criminal outcomes such as assault. Cummins reports on the qualitative indices, such as client feedback, that he has gathered post-treatment, and they suggest success in terms of personal insight gained from participation in his group therapy. Horley and Johnson (2008) have collected some limited data on a treatment group for domestic abusers. They found that the self-esteem of male abusers, as measured by a self-ideal discrepancy, increased over the course of a 12-week program, although the significance of this finding on future abusive behaviour is debatable.

The significance of common therapist-client constructions to therapeutic success has been argued (see Landfield, 1975). Rowe (1971) examined the accuracy of a psychiatrist's understanding of his client's constructs, where the rep grid provided a measure of the dimensions of misunderstanding between therapist and client. A client generated eight bipolar constructs and was provided with an additional seven. The psychiatrist was given the same set of constructs and elements. While Rowe's psychiatrist showed a reasonable degree of insight into the client's construct system, he did make some systematic errors. A similar study (Watson, 1970b) was extended over a nine-month period during which a therapist and client completed four identical rep grids. The results were very similar to Rowe's results in that the therapist had a reasonable understanding of the client but relatively little insight into the client's use of several constructs.

Fransella and Joyston-Bechal (1971) examined a therapy group using the grid in order to study changes in the patterning of ideas and to identify group process in both the patients and therapists. Caplan *et al.* (1975) correlated clients' grids with behavioural indicies, such as participation during group sessions, and processes occurring during therapy. They found that individual participation and the level and type of verbal activity of the group as a whole affected the ratings on the grid. They noted that the grid can present difficulty in analysis because it is a problem distinguishing unreliable measurement from valid indications of change. Shapiro *et al.* (1975) suggested combining information from other sources, such as the Personal Questionnaire and verbal behaviour, to assist with interpreting results. Fielding (1975) used the rep grid in combination with the Symptom Check List Rating Scale as a measure of outcome of group therapy.

A study of marital success and construct congruence of couples found no relationship between the number of shared constructs and marital adjustment (Weigel *et al.*, 1973). However, the dimensions used were 40 supplied constructs rather than personal constructs. The researchers concluded that marital success may relate more to the ability to predict the partner's construct system than to shared constructs.

Fransella (1968) used the rep grid to look at the self-concepts of stutterers. She found that people who stutter do not conceptualize themselves as stutterers. Instead, they see stutterers in the same sort of way that speech experts and laypeople do. On a grid with photographs as elements and with supplied constructs, there was no significant correlation between the construct "like me in character" and "stutterer". Fransella proposed that therapy should endeavour to help the stutterer accept stuttering as part of his or her true self and then help the patient build up a system of constructs to do with him or herself as a person who speaks normally. The dichotomy between self and behaviour found with stutterers also appears in the grids of alcoholics. Orford (1974) used the rep grid to study the construing of alcoholics. He examined early drop-out from an alcoholism halfway house in terms of cognitive complexity/simplicity in construing other people. Orford's measures of simplicity involved unipolarity of free descriptions and grid redundancy. He found some support for the hypothesis that individuals with relatively simple constructions of others tend to leave treatment sooner than more complex individuals.

One area of more recent concern within PCT has been sex therapy. Winter (1988, 2005) described cases where a personal construct approach appeared effective in addressing psychogenic impotence and other sexual issues for particular clients. The thrust of the treatment concerned exploration of core constructs, as well as clients' views of ongoing relationships. Winter (2005) has argued that, despite no research on efficacy, PCT be used more often by sex therapists because of its wholistic approach and technical eclecticism.

Viney *et al.* (2005) concluded that there appears to be "encouraging evidence of the effectiveness of personal construct psychotherapy" (p. 363). Included here would be recent work with offenders that has been, in general, effective (Horley, 2005b). FRT with forensic clients, even difficult cases, can be effective as evidenced by a number of single-case experiments (e.g., Horley, 2005a). These results will be discussed below, along with a description of some PCT approaches to therapy with sex offenders.

Individual psychotherapy with sexual offenders

Fixed-role therapy

Fixed-role therapy (FRT) was introduced by Kelly (1955). FRT has been described and elaborated since Kelly's introduction by Bonarius (1970), Epting (1984), and Winter (1992a), among others. FRT is a dramaturgical approach to psychotherapy, based loosely on some of the early writings of Moreno (1934/1978), an interesting innovator in many areas of psychology (Horley and Strickland, 1984) who proposed two forms of psychotherapy, psychodrama and sociodrama, based on formal role playing. According to Kelly, the client can restructure his or her construct system by considering and enacting new roles. In FRT, a client is asked to adopt a "new personality" in the form of a fixed sketch of a character at odds in particular dimensions from his or her current troubled self. The emphasis is placed on a thematic shift rather than the correction of minor personal problems. By acting out a new and more functional role, important change to the client should be manifested over time, although Epting *et al.* (2003) suggested that the point of FRT is demonstrating that personal change is possible.

Developing an acceptable personality sketch is the task of the therapist only after assessment of the client, which includes considerable understanding of the nature of the person that the client would like to become. The sketch, rarely if ever representing an ideal individual, is presented to the client with "the full protection of 'make-believe'" (Kelly, 1955, p. 373), which means that the client is asked to engage in a creative endeavour rather than an attempt to become what he or she should be or what the therapist desires. The client is encouraged, via discussion around character development and role playing, to see the world through the eyes of the new character. In contrast to Kelly (1955), who suggested that FRT could be viewed as a form of short-term or brief therapy with some extension for more difficult cases, I would suggest that it be viewed as a much more extended project when involving violent offenders well socialized into criminal roles. Kelly, it must be accepted, worked primarily with university students showing relatively minor adjustment problems.

Interestingly, FRT has been used with criminal offenders for a considerable time. In one of the first reports, Skene (1973) discussed the treatment of a "case of homosexuality" using FRT. Homosexuality in the late 1960s would have been interpreted in many jurisdictions as a sexual offense, although it is unclear whether Skene's client was attracted to pubescent or prepubescent males. At any rate, Skene reports the successful "reorientation" (i.e., heterosexual interests and acts) of the client following some months of FRT.

Various forensic therapists (e.g., Houston, 1998; Horley, 2003b) have argued that FRT should be used in more forensic treatment settings, especially involving complex and difficult cases. I (Horley, 2005a) demonstrated the effectiveness of FRT in a single-case experiment involving a sexual offender. Clients with multiple paraphilias, which appear fairly common (Adams and McAnulty, 1993), might be very appropriate candidates. Unravelling and treating the various sexual difficulties of some individuals presents a daunting task, especially when such individuals often demand wholesale change yet offer few personal insights. The ability to help a client address various problems at once, as opposed to dealing with each separately then combining the outcomes to examine possible interactions, is important. Dramaturgical approaches like FRT may not suit all clients, but many forensic clients are experienced in "confidence games" and may well accept a role-playing challenge in therapy. This would allow a therapist to focus on building existing personal strengths rather than concentrating on overcoming personal weaknesses (see Roesch, 1988).

One difficulty with FRT for sexual offenders involves developing effective fixed-role sketches (i.e., ones that the client can relate to in terms of a workable ideal). Often ideals for offenders – perhaps less so for many sexual offenders who do not express as many antisocial sentiments as other offenders – are difficult to relate to for therapists (i.e., may involve drug abuse, sexual variation, aggression, or other antisocial aspects). To write an effective sketch, however, the client's ideal (usually expressed in "ideal self sketch" format) needs to be considered seriously. The sketch writer needs to avoid unworkable roles (i.e., those perhaps construed as "straights", "square Johns", or simply "not me, never could be"). Having an experienced "characterization coach" (e.g., a therapeutic aide or prison trustee, an experienced colleague) to help rough out the basic sketch can be useful. Also, significant feedback from the client is required while "testing" the new character. If a very prosocial character with no "rough edges" is foisted on the client, it will likely result in rejection, either explicit (e.g., "Forget it, this isn't anyone I can relate to!") or implicit (e.g., "I'm trying, but it's tough getting my head around this guy.").

Another difficulty with FRT in a prison setting, or even certain community-based forensic settings (e.g., half-way house), is limitation of experimentation of the new role. The social and physical environmental conditions of most prisons do not permit the range of experiences that allow for "behavioural try-outs" of new actions based on new ways of construing. Often, poor substitutes are all that would be available for a client in a prison (e.g., talking to a female guard in an appropriate manner in place of asking a female love interest for a date). In many cases where only poor substitutes were available, especially in maximum-secure facilities, I have relied on "imaginary encounters" and substantial discussion of how the new "personality" would respond or think.

One critical point to consider when developing and presenting fixed-role sketches is the forensic setting. Some sketches could result in a client's victimization if enacted in the wrong place, and some prisons are completely the wrong place for someone attempting to become more sensitive to others or concerned about a neighbour's well-being. The "inmate code", or the unwritten yet prescribed set of acceptable behaviours for prison inmates, needs to be considered. This varies somewhat from facility to facility, but sexual offenders in any facility, even some forensic hospitals, need to conform to the code, especially given their lowly status in the inmate hierarchy. A prudent approach would be to go over the new sketch in detail with the client, in extreme detail about possible negative outcomes of implied behaviours from the sketch, expressing warnings wherever necessary. On more than one occasion, I have found it necessary to send a sketch "home" (i.e., to the street upon release) with a client with a stern warning "Don't try this here". Feedback can then be provided through phone conversations, letters, "anonymous" communications, or contacts through community-based probation-parole officers or therapists. While this situation is far from ideal, dealing with the frustration on both sides is better than dealing with the death or severe injury that may result from trying to be too therapeutic in an extremely non-therapeutic setting.

As well as increased quantity of therapy, many offenders appear to need increased intensity and focus of therapy than other clients. Much of my time in FRT with offenders is spent in encouragement and character elaboration/definition rather than role playing. Whether this is a result of high need for planning and specificity, or perhaps a need to know the new character very well so that role change is facilitated, is difficult to know. In some cases, the few if any prosocial models available any time throughout their lives mean that more character expansion and support for prosocial thoughts and actions are required. Incarcerated offenders' division of their social worlds into pro versus antisocial aspects appears to be relatively common, at least among clients in maximum-secure institutions (see Horley, 2005b). It is also a very difficult view of the social world to alter if only because it is a very adaptive construal pattern behind prison walls. By virtue of "black versus white" simplicity, it promotes preemptive construal insofar as a person can become a "rat-and-nothing-but-a-rat", or whatever construct seems appropriate at the time. This, in turn, fosters instant, unequivocal responses in a situation where equivocation can be fatal. There is little circumspection or consideration of alternatives in prisons because, at the very least, hesitation is perceived as weakness, and the weak do not survive in the daily dog-eat-dog world of many contemporary prisons. Perhaps the best way around this problem, short of a complete change to the prison environment, which might not be a bad idea (see Horley and Bennett, 2003), is to offer FRT just prior to release. This approach to psychotherapy, typical in some institutions because of limited therapeutic resources, can permit a view of "softness" or "weakness" of therapy clients by other inmates as the result of "shaking rough" due to an impending release.

An apparent difficulty with FRT concerns the honing of offenders' acting abilities. Some clinicians may be worried that FRT would allow forensic clients to cover existing pathologies or dupe potential victims more effectively by becoming better actors. This concern, for me, is more apparent than real because the effort is going into a single, prosocial character enactment. From a PCT perspective, the "pathology" is not seen as some deep, innate aspect of the person but an alterable – albeit with much effort in some cases – psychological set of constructs. This fear may be expressed whenever strengths of an offender rather than deficits are called into play during any form of therapy that builds on strengths. We, as clinicians, may fear doing more harm than good by allowing an individual with problems to take charge of their own improvement by building on existing abilities. What we need to keep in mind is that, however damaged the individual, almost all have some redeeming or positive features. It is clearly a possibility that the new character will be added to a "character collection" by skilled confidence artists to be brought out at certain times during the commission of future attempts to dupe unsuspecting victims. Because there are no guarantees about clients' true motives for improvement, either at the time of treatment or later, we need to accept this as simply one possible if undesirable outcome.

The principles and practice of FRT are established (Kelly, 1955; Epting, 1984). Horley (2005a, 2006) and Houston (1998) have reported on the use of FRT with offenders. It appears that FRT should be examined in more forensic treatment settings, especially involving more complex and difficult cases. The ability to help a client address various problems at once as opposed to dealing with each separately then combining the outcomes to examine interactions, is important. Dramaturgical approaches like FRT may not suit all clients but, since many sex offender clients are experienced in "confidence games", they may accept and even thrive on a role-playing approach to therapy. This approach might be advantageous in that it emphasizes the development of existing strengths, versus the elimination of personal weaknesses, of forensic clients (Roesch, 1988).

The case of Al

Al was a 25-year-old when we first met in a maximum-security prison. He was serving a sentence of several months for drug offenses. His drug of choice was cocaine, and he was a regular drug user and occasional trafficker. His record included a number of minor assault convictions. In fact, he had been classified to maximum security because of institutional violence. In spite of his violent tendencies, Al was very outgoing and rather well liked by both inmates and staff. According to Al, despite a hair-trigger temper, he liked to "keep it light" as much as possible while incarcerated.

Al was from a poor working-class family, raised by a single mother who worked at a number of menial jobs to support her son and daughter in an impoverished section of a large city. Al reported that he was in trouble with authorities frequently as a youth, complaining that he was frequently "fingered" simply because he was from "the wrong side of the tracks". He suggested that his anger and drug abuse stemmed from his early experiences with unforgiving and unfair authorities. Al had no prior convictions for sexual assault, yet he came to me because, he said, he had been having some very disturbing dreams and sexual fantasies. He was a very active bisexual, and had found himself attracted sexually to a recently incarcerated serial sexual killer. He reported that his fantasies and dreams were becoming increasingly violent, centering on the serial killer's activities, and he was concerned that he was "going down the same road as . . . [the serial killer]". He requested psychophysiological assessment of his sexual preferences and, while he did show a response to both male and female adults, he revealed no interest in either sexual or non-sexual violence. This may have been a reflection of a relatively low-level problem (i.e., he was only fantasizing about sexual violence rather than acting on his fantasies), although it must be recognized that he could have invented the problem in order to gain access to a therapist. Whatever the case, I took his concerns seriously, and we began a round of psychological assessment.

Al completed a self-characterization sketch (Kelly, 1955), in which he described himself as a fun-loving yet angry individual. While he viewed himself as a loving individual, he questioned whether he had ever "really loved . . . I hurt people I care about by putting my negative caring needs for myself first . . . I care first about dope, sex, and money". Al's involvement in psychotherapy to date was limited to an institutional anger management group. He did not believe that he had been helped, and he pleaded that he needed help immediately and intensively. We decided on individual therapy, and I suggested FRT for a number of reasons. First, he was sociable and he was usually skillful in social situations. Also, he always seemed to be involved in gamesmanship (e.g., gaining favours from other inmates or prison authorities). Perhaps more significantly, he recognized some of the destructive roles that he played around others, usually involving attempts to manipulate and control them. He was very comfortable around his sister, he said, because she allowed him to "play himself". Also, he demanded a "real transformation" in a period of several weeks. We met as often as possible, usually every couple of days, in individual sessions. Together, we created an alternative role, Aron. Aron was a very sociable individual who enjoyed parties, including alcohol and marijuana consumption, but knew his limits. He was confident, self-assured, and tended to be very assertive but not aggressive. Most importantly, Aron was very self-controlled especially concerning negative emotional expression.

Al accepted Aron and appeared to view adoption of the character as a personal challenge. He needed much prompting and discussion about the basis of his confidence (i.e., what a person who was truly confident would think and feel) but his active participation in the therapeutic process made our sessions very productive. One change that I noticed during his remaining incarceration was that Al, perhaps as Aron, managed to control his anger and did not have any further institutional assaults. He reported that he was discovering that words could persuade someone to comply with his wishes faster than his fists. My last contact with Al, and he seemed very keen to keep in touch, was about a year after his release. He had not reoffended and had begun sessions with a counsellor. Although he had not dealt completely with drug abuse, he was optimistic that he was heading in the right direction. We lost contact, unfortunately, and his long-term success is unknown.

Cognitive restructuring

By far the most important and frequent form of individual therapy that I provided to sex offenders in maximum-security facilities was what was termed "cognitive restructuring". This term was used in part because offenders saw it as a popular type of treatment and, perhaps more importantly, it was a non-threatening term. The professional problem with the term is connection with rationalist forms of psychotherapy (e.g., Ellis, 1962), but I tend to use the term cognitive in a broad sense (see Horley, 2000) so as not to raise objections from constructivists like Kelly (1955).

This form of individual psychotherapy is appropriate for situations where FRT or enactment therapies are difficult to use (e.g., maximum-secure facilities) or when clients object to enactment-based approaches. Cognitive restructuring can be an elaborative technique as described by Winter (1992a). A client is invited to identify and explore his own construct system by way of "talking about yourself, your past, and how you think about things". This process inevitably involves addressing a client's inconsistencies, construct system fragments or subsystems, and personal concerns, with the intent of allowing him to resolve inconsistencies and to elaborate personal meaning. Clearly there can be some "slot rattling" involved, but I do not see changing the use of a particular construct as necessarily insignificant when it comes to personal understanding. Reconstruing oneself as "thoughtful" versus "thoughtless" when the outcome might be not raping versus raping another individual is not trivial.

Challenging accounts or understandings of one's life and actions are part of the process of cognitive restructuring but, because this is not a rationalistic therapy, there is no "name calling" or "finger pointing" with respect to a client's account of events. Indeed, much of my effort in this individual work is spent examining and, in many cases, attempting to disabuse the client of many negative labels or "names" that others, especially therapists, have placed on him (e.g., homosexual pedophile, psychopath, paranoid schizophrenic). Use of guilt in the Kellian sense, and even displacement from "negative" core roles (e.g., "solid con"), can be an important tool in getting an offender to reconstrue himself and relations with others. What is vital is that the offender is allowed to express himself (i.e., his views are respected) and is given hope for change, accepting that both respect and hope are experienced all too seldom in many prisons.

One potential problem in cognitive restructuring involves self-pity. Due to the abuse and violence, emotional as well as physical, of typical forensic settings, and in part due to the victimization experienced by many sexual offenders, there is a tendency to indulge in self-pity and the construction or reconstruction of oneself as victim. This is a difficult line to walk, but allowing a client to express feelings of victimization is important while at the same time keeping the present concern of "self as victimizer" salient for the client. This can be maintained by pointed questions and comments, and in general by keeping discussion focussed on the problems at hand. Often personal abuse experiences that require further attention can be handled by telling the client that such issues can be dealt with "on the outside" or with another therapist.

The problem of self-pity involves a larger issue of "directiveness" in this therapy. While the client must be left to tell his story and express his perspective, antisocial statements cannot go unchallenged lest silence be construed as validation, and many sex offenders are adept at finding or extorting validation. As described by a number of authors (e.g., Andrews and Bonta, 1998), the most effective forensic counsellors appear to be firm in accepting only prosocial comments. This may seem to compromise a complete acceptance of a client's perspective that PCT posits (Chin-Keung, 1988; Winter and Watson, 1999), but the therapist must also consider the "other", whether a victim or any potential victim (i.e., all members of society), in a therapeutic encounter. Challenges do not have to be abrupt verbal assaults (e.g., "You're wrong there!"), but can be requests to examine particular statements (e.g., "Do you really believe that women like rough sex and like to be forced?"). The distinction here may be fine but important.

The case of Roberto

Roberto was in his early forties when we first met in a maximum-secure prison in Canada. He had been born in the United States. He was the second youngest child in a large family who lived and farmed in a rural area. The only member of his family he reported being close to while growing up was his younger sister. His father he saw as an abusive alcoholic, while he remembered his mother as domineering and overbearing. Even his older brother and sisters were recalled as hateful and violent. He wet his bed as a child until he was nearly a teenager because, he said, his life at home was so stressful. Roberto saw many of the family's problems rooted in alcohol abuse, and he admitted that he had been a problem drinker since his mid-teens. He also abused street drugs, mostly marijuana.

He was arrested as a youth for drug possession, criminal trespass, and breach of peace. These seemed like relatively minor offenses until he revealed that the breach was actually a plea bargain for a sexual offense involving a ten-year-old boy that occured when he was 17 years of age. He also admitted that he had been arrested about the same time for an indecent act, exhibiting his genitals to "a group of kids" in the neighbourhood, which led to a fine. During all this time, the only help that he received came in the form of six months of weekly counselling sessions from a church minister. According to Roberto, the only benefit he received from the counselling was the support of the minister, who arranged for him to attend a local university, where he graduated with a bachelor's degree four years later. The degree, in a sense, provided more trouble because it allowed him to teach in a primary school and exposed him to young male students. He committed another sexual offense involving a young male, was arrested, and served two years in a state prison. On his release, he married but continued to have sexual relationships with young males, one of which led to another conviction, although he fled the country before sentencing in the case.

His life in Canada, while on the run from U.S. justice, involved a series of relationships with women, but always including some sexual contact with young males. He was eventually charged, convicted, and sentenced to two years in a Canadian prison for a number of offenses involving the "sexual touching" of a series of prepubescent males. According to Roberto, he never hurt or forced any boy to do anything that "didn't feel good". He was, however, keen to receive help to "discontinue" his sexual involvements with boys. He stated that "I really don't want to hurt others for my own gratification but to paraphrase a Bible verse 'That which I try to do, I do not. That which I try not to do, that I do.' I love kids and don't want to hurt them in any way but I seem to hurt them anyway." He agreed to weekly individual sessions with me, and I suggested cognitive restructuring. Roberto agreed so long as the therapy would give him "the proper skills" to avoid sexual contact with minors.

A series of pre-treatment assessments, including penile plethysmography, revealed relatively little useful information, at least until he completed a rep grid. His grid results (see Figure 5.1) seemed to confirm what he had told me repeatedly; namely, he was a loner and felt that, despite many relationships with many individuals, both young and old, he was desperately isolated. The more he tried to reach out to others, the more he felt himself cut off from others. According to the factor analysis of his rep grid, the closest figure he saw to himself was his ideal self, followed by the boy. It was interesting that he saw himself in the extreme lower right quadrant of the graph, in the Caring and Immature area. For him, immature referred to age – and he described himself as young – as well as "not responsible", "careful of words", and "not able to share experiences by being male". Caring, on the other hand, seemed to refer to an individual who was a Christian, concerned with others, optimistic, and, rather interestingly, "same ethnic background".

This case may appear at first glance a classic from a Freudian (Freud, 1905/ 1975), or at least neo-Freudian perspective (Fraser, 1976), in the sense that a man with a cold and domineering mother and a relatively ineffectual father molests prepubescent boys in an attempt to address an unresolved Oedipal

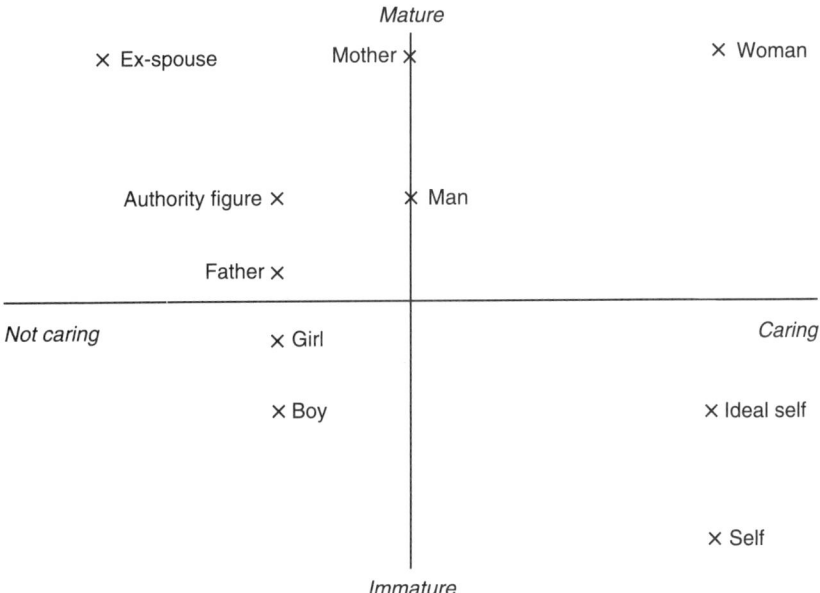

Figure 5.1 Results of Roberto's rep grid analysis (non-parametric factor analysis).

conflict. A better interpretation, however, appears available. Personal construct therapy in the form of cognitive restructuring consisted, first, of an exploration of Roberto's meanings concerning some of the terms that he used. He seemed somewhat perplexed, yet intrigued, by the results of his grid. We examined all the implications of his view of himself and his ideal as immature, and we discussed the relative closeness of the boy, which he did not find very surprising. We discussed the relationship for him between immaturity and sexual attraction, especially considering the placement of the woman, whom he respected yet was not attracted to sexually, in the top right quadrant, rather alone. Roberto admitted that, for him, freedom, lack of responsibility, and spontaneity were attactive qualities. He stated that children were attractive because they are "fun to be around, willing to try new things. Curious enough to try new stuff. Generally, honest and trusting". We discussed various meanings of immaturity in an attempt to have him reconstrue his understanding of immaturity, and what children in particular meant to him, as part of an effort to shift his ideal self, and perhaps later himself, to the top with the woman. Interestingly, he reported that he had been discovered by his parents with his younger sister "about 5 or 6 . . . showing each other what we had", and he remembered clearly during the shouting that followed being asked "What is wrong with you?" He accepted that it was possible that, at this point, he began to regard himself as somehow perverse or different.

Roberto's long-term involvement in the church, with an accompanying tendency to quote scripture, and a desire to construe in a categorical manner often made our sessions frustrating to me, but he remained open to possible reinterpretation of his understanding of himself and others. It would have been ideal to spend more than three months working with him given his degree of involvement with prepubescent males, but his transfer to face further charges meant that no second rep grid could be administered. His subsequent extradition to the United States also meant that follow-up of any sort with him was a practical impossibility.

Covert sensitization

Since initial development and introduction by Cautela (1966), covert sensitization as a therapeutic technique has been viewed as either strictly behavioural or cognitive-behavioural. I would suggest that it can be construed as constructivistic, albeit loosely so. The procedure involves having a client imagine a negative outcome to an event that typically involved positive outcomes. When involving sex offender clients, the technique is often used in conjunction with phallometric assessment as a form of sexual preference reassignment therapy (see Quinsey and Earls, 1990) when the client is aroused by a "negative stimulus" (e.g., a sexual assault). This does assume that a client is aroused by an inappropriate sexual object (e.g., prepubescent child) or activity (e.g., rape) which includes only a minority of sexual offenders. The client is briefed about his role in the session, and the therapist takes on the role of a "thought coach" who suggests a number of images or useful ideas. Tactics may expand beyond focussing on the negative outcomes of the imagined situation (e.g., disease, death, incarceration) to include the particular negative feelings and thoughts of the offender in the situation (e.g., embarrassment at return to prison). One approach that appears helpful is use of Kellian guilt in terms of helping the client see how he might feel if he were to engage in offensive acts inconsistent with existing or new core role constructs.

In my work with sex offenders, covert sensitization is useful in particular with developmentally delayed or brain-damaged clients, especially serious solvent and alcohol abusers. The procedure gives them a concrete act (viz., penile arousal to a negative event) and a relatively concrete connecting event. So long as the focus of the procedure is on thoughts or construal processes rather than on genital responses, the technique is available to constructivists. While a therapist may be altering sexual preference patterns by using such a procedure, the underlying change involves a construct shift reinforced or maintained by a negative event.

The case of Kevin

Kevin was a 28-year-old serving a two-year sentence for a breach of probation. The offense involved failure to comply with probation conditions related to remaining away from a schoolyard where children played. This probation order followed a lengthy penitentiary term for involvement in the death of a child. According to Kevin, he had a longstanding interest in children, and penile plethysmographic assessment revealed a marked sexual preference for prepubescent males. Intelligence testing supported the frequent mention in his personal file of "subnormal intelligence"; he seemed to have a mild developmental delay. Kevin had some difficulty in completing many psychological assessments, including the rep grid, and his reading ability was at a very low level.

Kevin claimed to be interested in intensive psychotherapy, yet he appeared unable to think abstractly, ruling out much cognitive therapy. He was quite prepared to engage in covert sensitization, and we proceeded using the plethysmographic laboratory. During each sensitization session, Kevin's penile responses to pictures depicting prepubescent males and adult females (his prefered adult targets) were monitored. He was instructed to try to respond only to the women and suppress responses to the boys and, to assist in the process, he was given a warning light to indicate when his sexual responses to a boy reached a predetermined level. Kevin reported on the nature of his sexual fantasies involving both boys and women at the beginning of our work together. He had very clear and elaborated fantasies involving boys, most involving an element of excitement or danger yet mutual respect and pleasure, whereas his fantasies involving women seemed to be rather uniform and banal. We discussed ways by which he could make the fantasies with boys less appealing (i.e., introduce negative images or elements) as well as means by which he could elaborate and increase the appeal of the fantasies involving women. Before each session I would review how he had done in the previous session and provide a summary of what he had reported had worked for him. After each session I would provide feedback on his results and ask about what he had been thinking or imagining during particular trials or slides.

At the beginning of our work together, Kevin responded moderately to boys but very little to the women, with a ratio of about five to one. He seemed to make slow but steady progress over the course of weekly sessions for a period of seven months, to the point where he managed to decrease responses to boys and increase responses to women to the point of a ratio of one to one. He still, as he said, "lost it" on occasion with the new pictures (slides of both boys and women were rotated every session) but, overall, did manage to develop control, at least in the lab setting. Although we were not discussing construction directly, he did appear to make the connection between pre-pubescent fantasies with "bad" and adult fantasies with "good" using various cognitive strategies that allowed him to respond less enthusiastically when it came to young boys. Whether he will be able to gain control over the long term in a community setting filled with real and undoubtedly appealing youngsters remains to be seen. He has remained in a semi-structured community setting (i.e., a half-way house for developmentally delayed adults) for a number of years without further sexual offenses, but he has been seeing a number of mental health specialists during the entire time. It may be that our work together was simply a first step for him to take, though I am sure that it was an important step nonetheless.

Personal projects therapy

The analysis of personal projects, these everyday activities intended to attain or maintain a particular state of affairs, has been notably silent on the improvement of lives via change in project construction or pursuit, at least until now. It appears to me that project analysis can lead to more effective lives, and therapists might want to consider the nature of a client's everyday involvements in terms of dysfunction and difficulty. The major concerns with the formulation, staging, and completion of everyday activities might centre around a number of issues.

One obvious issue with personal projects involves the construal of projects. If activities are viewed as highly desirable yet completely unattainable or extremely unpleasant, there should be little expectation of success. One avenue of intervention could focus on the reconstrual of particular activities, where, for example, "troublesome" is recast as "character-building challenge" or "too time consuming" is seen as "worth struggling for". This approach would be clearly constructivistic, but other modes or types of intervention are also possible.

Many valuable projects appear to be set in the wrong places and, as a result, have no or limited chance of successful completion. A project like "Stop smoking" set in a comfortable cigar lounge would undoubtedly go up in smoke. Moving a project, or the person with the project, to a more conducive place might help in conducting and, ultimately, completing the activity. From my experience with some probation and parole officers, especially highly effective ones who engage clients and are concerned with their everyday lives, this is precisely what they advise on. They discover what the client is engaged in, from looking for work to avoiding criminal involvement, and suggest places where such activities might be best launched or conducted.

It might also be the case that associates, or the pool of potential project assistants, is the source of project problems. No social support is a problem, but many offenders suffer from exposure to the wrong kind of support. "Finding a legal job" is a project doomed to failure if conducted around associates who sell cocaine or shoplift for a living. Again, good probation and parole workers unquestionably offer advice on this matter, not only in terms of avoiding criminal associates but in terms of seeking others who can provide real help with particular projects. People and places, without a question, populate the real world of projects. Discovering the most conducive people and places to facilitate activities is not always easy, particularly for released offenders who have few available resources, including information about help in a particular community. Often, long-term incarcerates have no one, including family members, to turn to for help with even the most basic projects.

I have used personal projects based interventions with a number of offender clients over the years, including sex offender clients. The response, to date, has been mixed. In some cases, the inability to imagine, or to imagine the absolute worst possible situation for some offenders makes entry into a therapuetic conversation about future projects difficult. With no or few concrete plans, at least not ones that they would be willing to share, many offenders have a bleak view of the world outside prison walls and, probably realistically based on previous experience, little optimism concerning their chances of success. In some cases, help with eliciting and elaborating various projects of limited scope (e.g., "Getting temporary work", "Keeping a journal") can start a process of reconsideration of the usual cycle of frustration and reoffense. Small steps with respect to post-release projects may be the best strategy for success.

My work with sexual offenders using personal projects has been greatly aided by the use of the personal project matrix (see previous chapter). In general, clients appear to grasp the idea of the personal project rather readily. They find the process of listing and considering various aspects of their everyday lives useful, perhaps because their life experiences are valued using this procedure and/or because the procedure is very concrete and pertains to everyday life events. The results of these efforts, however, have yet to be properly evaluated. No doubt preliminary trial and error, perhaps much error, has limited success in some cases, but I offer one case example for consideration.

The case of Paul

Paul was a 30-year-old individual who came to see me in a maximum-security prison. We had worked together during his previous incarceration, but his stay in the community lasted only a few weeks. I had been hopeful when Paul was released, as had he, but he returned quickly to his former life of drugs and violence. His convictions included manslaughter, various drug-related offenses, and sexual assault. He had spent almost all of the previous ten years behind bars. During his previous incarceration, he claimed to have "found God", and he wanted to banish "bad Paul" in favour of "good Paul". Unfortunately, despite both our efforts, "bad Paul" won.

I decided to try something different with Paul this time. He stated that he wanted to "get real" and "improve [him]self" in very specific ways. Although an intelligent individual, Paul was very concrete – he worked at mechanical trades when not selling drugs – and when we talked he preferred very tangible and specific examples. I told him that I wanted to examine the manner in which he organized his everyday activities and to see if, together, we could find better ways to initiate, to conduct, and to organize his personal projects. I gave him two forms of the Personal Project Analysis (PPA), one to complete in terms of his present projects while incarcerated and one to complete in terms of his anticipated projects in the community on release. The latter project matrix was intended to see what kinds of immediate plans he envisioned, and perhaps more importantly how, where, and with whom he expected to accomplish these projects.

Paul had no trouble completing the present PPA. Many of his projects tended to be solitary self-improvement activities, which was not too surprising given that Paul chose to complete his sentence away from other inmates in segregation – a suggestion that the authorities readily agreed with because of Paul's history of violence. These projects included "Recognizing my anger as it occurs", "Keeping my spiritual life in order", and "Being considerate of those around me". Even his interpersonal projects, such as "Maintaining close relationship with parents" and "Reworking my relationship with girlfriend", tended to be limited to a very select group of weekly visitors. He saw most of his activities as very important, self-initiated, within his own control, and highly likely to succeed. All of his projects, he readily admitted, were very lofty prosocial ones that he had in mind previously, yet had failed at miserably. One key to Paul's possible failure may have been that, with the exception of two interpersonal projects, he saw all of his current activities as very unlike him, generally 0 on a 0–10 rating scale. I pointed this out to him and, while he agreed that these projects were very atypical ones, at least in terms of what he did normally, he argued that they were the keys to his future success. While I noted that he may be casting the possibility of his own future failure by placing too much pressure on himself to succeed, we discussed how much he had accomplished over the past two years, and how these activities were not completely alien to him. My intention here was to nudge him towards a slightly more "prosocial self", one that might persevere with his personal choices rather than casting them aside as not only too stressful but "really not who I am anyway".

One issue that we considered at length concerned the lack of other people, in the form of "project assistants", involved in his projects. With the exception of his parents and current girlfriend, and he was not sure how secure that relationship would prove to be over the course of his incarceration, no one was involved in his projects. Paul believed that people tended to lead him astray or to abandon him, so he decided that he would "go it alone" during his present incarceration and on release. The lack of social support was extremely evident when I asked him to complete another PPA, but this time in the future, six months post-release. Some of his projects remained the same (e.g., working on relationships, controlling his temper, considering others) but there were some new and key additions. He anticipated "Finding new employment", "Spending a certain amount of time each day relaxing", and "Do my best to refrain from alcohol and drugs".

Interestingly, he saw all of these projects as solo efforts – no one would be involved in any of these activities with him. When questioned about this further, Paul suggested that success in all these endeavours would mean that he would be able to turn his life around, and therefore he needed to do it on his own. My suggestions that other individuals may be helpful in, for example, finding honest employment because of their knowledge of business needs notwithstanding, he held fast to his individualistic position that he alone would have to accomplish these projects. Further exploration of this issue revealed that his father, clearly someone he regarded as a very positive role model, was a "self-made man" who "didn't need anyone's help" on the farm that he owned and operated. Coupled with his view that he owed much of his present situation to "bad company", Paul appeared doomed to fail once again. We discussed other social resources that he might rely on when released (e.g., members of his new church community), but it was very difficult to know how much Paul really felt that he could open up and allow others into his life and personal projects. He was very much a man on his own, and one without any real confidants. Paul recognized his own antisocial aspects. Again, on the future PPA, he saw staying away from drugs and controlling his anger as very unlike himself, but believed that, with divine intervention, he could change. Whether that assistance would come in time one could only guess, but at least Paul managed over the two years following his release to avoid any further charges. After that I lost contact, and it is difficult to tell if checks with authorities draw a blank because the individual in question has truly changed, has moved to another jurisdiction, or has died.

Group psychotherapy with sexual offenders

Although the literature on group psychotherapy with sexual offenders is far from extensive, it does appear to be among the earliest treatment approaches employed with sexual offenders (see Cabeen and Coleman, 1961). Group therapy for sex offenders has been advocated for a number of reasons, including acceptance by a peer group and the "reassurrance" that results from "discussion of secret feelings and actions without fear of punishment" (Cabeen and Coleman, 1961, p. 125). More recently, Lothstein and Bach (2002) added other considerations, such as the ability of a group setting to allow participants to deal with "developmental arrests, and gender and masculinity conflicts while attaining genuine intimacy" (p. 503). Unfortunately, based on my observations, group therapy is often the choice of overworked therapists in settings, such as prisons, with very limited therapeutic resources because of its perceived efficiency.

A variety of different forms of group therapy has been developed and employed by PCT therapists (see Winter, 1992a), including work with sexual offenders (e.g., Houston and Adshead, 1993). Here, I will avoid a lengthy discussion of various forms of PCT-based group therapy and will instead focus on some of the specific approaches to group therapy that I have used with my sex offender clients. Obviously, however, there are many more approaches to group work that could be introduced with such clients.

Problem identification

Developed as a general first step for sexual offenders interested in some help with psychological problems, problem identification was designed to provide a supportive environment for sexual offenders to discuss their lives, personal difficulties, and construct systems in order to receive feedback from therapist(s) and peers. The term "problem identification" was chosen quite intentionally as a generic descriptor that would not identify participants as sexual offenders – as one participant expressed it, "Everyone has problems!" When followed by the term "group", however, it does result in an unfortunate acronym, PIG, which in some cases has stuck to group participants. Variations on the name have also left much to be desired in terms of acronyms.

The problem identification groups that I have conducted in prison settings are process-oriented groups planned as a first step rather than an end in itself. The group operates as a closed therapy group as opposed to an open group (i.e., no new members are admitted after the first week's meeting) in order to promote group cohesion and trust among participants. Clients, usually six to eight per group, are allowed to speak without fear of attack (i.e., there is no "hot seat", insults, physical contact), although questionning and challenge is encouraged. Each group member is permitted over two weeks (or eight hours of group time) to tell his life story in whatever manner is deemed appropriate. Some participants rely on rambling accounts of recent significant events while others, including one who produced a 400-plus-page autobiography, present a detailed and coherent account of their entire life to date. The focus of each story is left to each participant to decide on his own.

The group composition that seems to work best is a homogeneous one with respect to offense and personal background. In fact, the more homogeniety the better (e.g., all middle-aged, middle-class, white males with offenses involving prepubescent male victims). One pitfall with this homogeniety concerns "alliances", or collections of individuals who relate so well that they band together to support each other. While this is a real danger insofar as allies can and do validate each other's deviant perspectives, it can be countered by challenges to all potential allies at the first sign of such a forma- tion. In extreme cases of unbreakable alliances, I have had to move a key member of the alliance to the next group or, in one case where a participant formed an alliance in order to support his verbal attacks on me, a participant can simply be removed from the group entirely.

A problem with any form of group psychotherapy with sex offenders, especially in a correctional institution, is fear of physical retribution by virtue of being identified as a sex offender. This is minimized by the generic and relatively benign title of this group, but the issue of confidentiality of information is important in any group such as this. The main intent of this group is to allow individuals to examine and to "troubleshoot", usually in very preliminary ways, their construct systems. As such, this group func- tions as an elaborative forum in a PCT sense. A very comfortable environ- ment is required (e.g., couches, dim lighting). Dropouts from this group – to date, usually less than 25 per cent – seem to result from an inability of indi- viduals to feel secure enough with other participants and/or therapists to participate.

Once again, this group format has yet to be evaluated in a formal, system- atic manner. While debriefing each participant after every final session of the group, I have encountered a range of comments. The main short-term bene- fits of this group approach to treatment appear to include a sense of not being alone. A number of participants have remarked that, until involvement in the group, they felt as if they alone had their particular sexually anomolous behaviour. Along with a sense of not being alone, the group seemed to foster a sense of hope concerning the ability to change. They witnessed some minor changes in other participants, and some reported noticing changes in their own thoughts and feelings as well. Participants often expressed an appreci- ation for being able to talk about themselves and have their personal stories heard and appreciated by others. Many participants in problem identification proceed to further therapy groups or to individual psychotherapy.

Relapse prevention

Relapse prevention is a popular form of therapy, typically in group format, borrowed from the alcohol treatment area and used by various therapists, including those who work with sex offenders (see Laws, 1989). It is described as a cognitive-behavioural approach to helping clients recognize how and why problem behaviours occur and how to avoid repetition. The language or jargon of relapse prevention is extensive, and aspects of different programs do vary, but I will present my variation of relapse prevention without limited jargon.

The relapse prevention group that I have operated for sexual offenders in a prison setting involves biweekly meetings over a 12-week period. Usually it involves a single therapist or group leader and between six and ten participants. Because the format tends to be didactic with open discussion, it will certainly accommodate more participants, and I have heard of some prison-based relapse groups with two dozen or more participants. Most individuals become involved in this group just prior to release, and I view it more as an opportunity to consolidate gains made throughout prior aspects of rehabilitation during incarceration.

A number of topics, typically a single one per session, are presented to the group for discussion. One issue for consideration concerns the notion of offense chains, or the chains of events that preceed a sexual offense. Each participant is encouraged to think back on his last sexual offense and identify each event that led up to the offense. By doing so – and I intentionally avoid the term "offense cycles" because of the connotation of inevitability and repetition – insight into the particular sequence of events that can produce an offense is promoted. Although sometimes a separate discussion, the idea of a high-risk situation is often introduced here, and participants attempt to identify for them the types of situations that might lead to reoffense. The notion of a "red flag", or warning point/event, is introduced so that the participants, by identifying their personal flags for the future, can be aware of cues that serve to warn them about the likely unacceptable series of events to follow. In a sense, this is an empowering exercise insofar as personal understanding and acceptance that everyone has choices to make at various times that have clear consequences.

Another concern of my relapse group is the nature of negative emotion. This usually follows offense chaining because most participants can identify at least one negative emotional link in the chain of their latest offense. The nature of negative affect in general, common negative feelings experienced by individual participants, and adaptive ways of coping with negative affect are some of the issues discussed. Ways of coping appropriately often lead into a discussion of natural helping networks. This issue always involves some advice on the development of social support and also how to provide effective help to those in need. Awareness of mutuality, sometimes a revelation for group participants, is important to avoid asking for help because of a perception that a debt is created because offenders have nothing to give in return.

One issue that I cover, but only briefly, concerns victim impact and the development of empathy. This usually involves a videotaped interview with a victim of sexual assault talking about the personal impact of the attack. Group participants are then requested to compose a letter of apology over the next two or three days in the privacy of their cells to their last victims, explaining how they now feel but focussing on the likely feelings of the victim himself or herself. The reason that I am less than keen on empathy training is that I regard it less as a simple social skill to be acquired readily through trial and error and reinforcement and more as a highly complex personal ability that is the result of significant early childhood experiences involving accurate reading and experience of others' affective experience. I doubt that an adult who has never been concerned about others' feelings can be taught to be empathic, at least not without significant and prolonged effort. This does not mean, however, that they are condemned to a lifetime of sex offenses because many non-empathic people never commit sexual assaults.

My emphasis in relapse prevention is not on behaviour per se or on the didactic information to prevent reoffense. Learning content is not important for me as a relapse group therapist. Rather, the discussions about thoughts and feelings, explorations of self, and understanding how particular events can produce specific important personal reactions are a central theme throughout the group meetings. This form of group therapy permits participants to explore how their own constructions of the world can lead directly to inappropriate actions in a setting where they can receive prompting as well as support. Participants' changing views of people and the world can then lead to new behavioural experiments, both within prison walls and in the broader community on release. All too often, relapse prevention becomes a lecture or even harangue about the obvious cues that offenders are unable or unwilling to recognise in order to avoid negative behaviours. Lecturing and berating offenders, whether in a group or individually, is not therapeutic and unlikely to lead to personal change. A group like relapse prevention needs to proceed with respect for the construal processes of all individuals.

Although not formally evaluated, I have always debriefed my relapse prevention participants at the completion of the group. The comment about the group that I have heard most often is that the men appreciate the specific examples of personal cues that they need to watch out for. With these insights, they often report feeling more prepared for life outside the institution than in times past, although their actual long-term success in the community remains to be determined.

Chapter 6

Assessment and treatment of sexual offenders

An illustrative case

Much of what I have presented in this book emphasizes the importance of individual analysis of each case. It seems important, therefore, to present a detailed single case of a sexual offender with whom I worked. There are a number of issues that I wish to highlight in this chapter. Most concern assessment decisions and related issues. Some of these issues and questions extend far beyond narrow PCT considerations.

The case that I have chosen is neither a spectacular success nor a spectacular failure. This case has not been published or even referred to in any of my published works. It is, in short, just a very ordinary case involving an incarcerated sexual offender, who I will call Pascal. Although this case garnered significant local media coverage at the time of the trial and when Pascal was released from prison, his criminal record is neither extensive nor remarkable. This case is likely similar to many encountered by forensic mental health professionals. Despite being more than ten years old, I recall the case very clearly; in fact, at times my notes seem unnecessary. One journalist managed to acquire at least one of my confidential reports and made my life difficult in the maximum-secure prison where I worked at the time. This was just one in a long sequence of experiences that convinced me to return to an academic setting, at least for a few years. No doubt Pascal's life in the community where he had settled following his release from custody was complicated as well by the media attention. My file on this case, in more ways than one, has never really been closed. Discussion of this case in the context of this book is an opportunity to reflect on some of these issues.

Pascal's background

Pascal was born the second son in a rural, working-class family that eventually included four children. His parents separated before he was five years old, and Pascal was removed temporarily to live in foster care. He spent the next ten years of his life shuffling between foster homes, group homes, and his father's home. He lived there with his father, one of a series of his father's live-in girlfriends, and one or two of his siblings. Although the family could not be described as desperately poor, money and other resources were scarce. Stability, in particular, was in short supply for Pascal during his early years. The only person he seemed to have any stable, long-term relationship with was his paternal grandmother. She was relatively involved in his life and seemed to stand up for him. Unfortunately, she lived on her own in a rural community in a distant part of the province.

As a child, Pascal committed two acts of arson. Neither resulted in personal injury, but both caused serious enough damage to attract the attention of the authorities. One fire, and possibly both, targeted a current or former girlfriend of his father. After the second incident, Pascal was declared a Crown Ward and sent into foster care on a full-time basis. He had earlier been found to have a serious learning disability and was not doing well in school. He had reported to a social worker, too, that he was often depressed and contemplated suicide, which resulted in years of continuous antidepressant medication. At least two incidents termed "suicide attempts" – they involved some form of self-harm – were listed in his file material.

Pascal's first sexual assault occurred when he was in his mid-teens. He fondled a younger girl at school, causing no physical harm, and school authorities did not involve the police. Later the same year, he fondled a prepubescent male in the change room of a local athletic club. Although police were called, no charges resulted. After a two-year period of relative calm, Pascal was arrested for the assault of a female teenager. He had attacked her in a public place, and released her when she screamed. Given his past record, he was charged, convicted of a sexual assault, and sentenced to a custodial sentence in a youth detention facility to be followed by a probation order. Soon after his release from the youth centre, he committed a series of sexual assaults that can only be characterized as bizarre and very worrying at the same time. These offenses resulted in charges, convictions, and a two-year prison term followed by several years of probation. The victims in these assaults ranged from a male toddler to three female teenagers. At no time did penetration occur or was even attempted, and Pascal did not attempt to flee from the scenes of any of the assaults. He reportedly expressed surprise that anyone found his actions inappropriate, even the teenaged girl knocked from her bike in a public roadway and partially disrobed. It was noted in various reports that Pascal, a rather large and muscular young man and apparently a large boy as well, could have killed any of his victims easily but he only employed enough physical intimidation to overcome resistance. Given credit for some of the circumstances described previously, Pascal was ordered on conviction to serve his relatively brief custodial sentence in a treatment centre to take advantage of psychological services and a sex offender treatment program in particular. While the court recognized the seriousness of these offenses, Pascal was viewed plainly as a troubled young man in need of some serious help.

My rather brief time with Pascal began after his transfer to the maximum-secure prison where I worked. He had spent several months at the nearby treatment centre involved in two therapy groups for sexual offenders, but during his time at the centre he had accumulated three institutional misconducts for a variety of "low-level incidents". He apparently displayed flashes of anger to both guards and treatment staff, refusing direct orders but never assaulting anyone, whether staff or inmate. The centre, however, maintained strict policies about conduct, or misconduct, so Pascal was sent to the only facility that could accommodate a relatively high-profile sex offender. He was also interested in applying for parole despite his record, criminal and institutional, so he came to see me immediately on admission for a set of assessments to serve as the basis of a report that needed to be sent to the relevant parole board.

Assessment results

Pascal's presentation during our first few assessment sessions was unremarkable. He seemed friendly and cooperative, if a bit reluctant to provide detailed answers to the questions that I asked him. Despite my caution about his chances for an early release, he seemed optimistic and very keen to see his father, with whom he planned to live, and his grandmother. His siblings, it seemed, had no more contact with him and he rarely saw his mother. He was quite willing to not only do what needed to be done for the parole assessment, but he also wanted to continue with treatment for the time he had remaining in custody. He became involved in a social skills group and started working in a prison factory position almost immediately. Fitting in to new and potentially unpleasant surroundings – this was his first experience in an adult, maximum-secure facility – seemed to present no problems to Pascal. He took everything that was thrown at him in his stride, including the denial of his parole application.

As expected, given his history of sexual offenses, there were a number of reports concerning specialized assessments conducted in the past. Penile plethysmographic assessments conducted at two different facilities at two different times revealed the same low-level and uninterpretable results. They could determine nothing about his sexual preference pattern. My concerns about the effects of antidepressants on his sexual functioning were waved off by Pascal who claimed to have no difficulty in that domain, so we attempted to repeat the testing in our psychophysical assessment laboratory. After two attempts, using audiotapes and videotapes of both consenting and non-consenting encounters involving children and adults, I gave up. Again, he showed no recordable sexual responses to any stimuli presented to him. He reported, indeed appeared, to be relaxed about the procedure, but he found none of the stimuli sufficiently arousing.

Following a failed attempt to collect information using a psychophysical technique, we proceeded to psychometric assessment. I asked him to complete a rep grid, and he agreed, but after many questions about the procedure and two or three abortive attempts to begin, Pascal became frustrated and handed the material back to me. I found this a bit surprising, having used the rep grid with "moderately retarded" and very thought disordered clients in the past with little problem. Earlier intellectual testing showed Pascal's results in the "normal intelligence" range, but barely. Thus, while he may have a learning disability and be marginal in terms of intelligence, he did not appear to be severely incapacitated in terms of mental ability. I have had a number of previous clients who did not complete the rep grid in the past, but it was usually a case of being unwilling to do it as opposed to unable to understand it. For instance, one of my first clients was an individual with a master's degree in business administration, very clever and cagey, who was serving a life sentence for murdering a business partner (admittedly not too clever). He looked the grid over for a few minutes and handed it back to me with a comment that he was not interested in completing a procedure that he could not understand in terms of "what was required . . . I don't know what you're looking for with this". Since then, I have been reasonably confident that the rep grid is not very transparent, which is valuable in use with forensic clients. I would add here that even when a client group or individual clients are likely to misrepresent themselves for obvious reasons, there is no reason to suspend a credulous approach to assessment. So long as we are aware that a client may lie, and take steps to expose lies or attempts to direct attention in other directions, we as forensic assessors and clinicians can proceed with a direct inquiry and may well glean important information from the lie or misdirection. Included here would be denials and minimization of responsibility that many sexual offenders employ in spades (see Barbaree, 1989; Horley, 2003a).

Pascal was requested to complete a self-characterization sketch. He spent some time at his autobiographical statement but produced very little information, a brief paragraph. Now, I suspected a real reluctance to participate fully in the assessment, and I turned to a technique of last resort. Despite sharing many concerns about the use of the Minnesota Multiphasic Personality Inventory (MMPI) discussed by several forensic clinicians (see Gendreau, 2002), I do use the technique on occasion, not because of the substantive scales based on the notion of pathological traits, but because it contains a full set of validity scales. I have found that the MMPI can be a valuable means of discovering and displaying to offenders attempts to dissemble or to withhold information. A brief discussion of the MMPI and its validity scales is required here.

Traditional psychological and psychiatric assessments are based on assumptions of honesty and accurate self-disclosure by test-takers (Rogers, 1997). The question of deception, whether defensiveness or "faking good" (i.e., attempting to represent oneself as normal when really suffering from pathology) or malingering or "faking bad" (i.e., attempting to represent oneself as pathological when really normal), is an important one for forensic mental health professionals. Aside from general justice and assessment accuracy issues, successful deception by forensic clients compromises two important areas of forensic mental health, cost of service and therapeutic efficacy. The cost of forensic services is a particular concern when clients attempt to represent themselves as pathological, requiring hospitalization and increased mental health attention. This becomes a serious economic consideration as forensic resources decrease and as per diem rate differentials between corrections and forensic hospitals increase. In addition, therapeutic efficacy is threatened when clients enter treatments unnecessarily and skew treatment outcomes, producing either "miraculous recoveries" or resistance to therapy (Greene, 1986), as deceptive clients continue attempts to misrepresent themselves and their conditions. All forensic mental health workers, particularly those involved in assessment procedures, have a responsibility to detect those who misrepresent their mental health conditions.

The MMPI, revised second edition (MMPI-2), is the most common paper-and-pencil test of psychopathology in forensic use today (Forbey and Ben-Porath, 2002), and it is also the most common psychological assessment of deception (Rogers *et al.*, 2003). It has become the standard by which other tests of deception are evaluated according to Butcher (1990). The 567 items on the MMPI-2 can produce scores on roughly 100 separate scales, including a number of validity scales. The scales that will provide a focus for the present discussion are the three oldest and most researched ones, the L, F, and K Scales (Forbey and Ben-Porath, 2002), although there are perhaps better "subtle" indices of malingering included within the MMPI-2 (see Greene, 1986).

The L or "Lie" Scale was originally designed to detect individuals who attempted to present themselves too favourably (Hathaway and McKinley, 1943), but Graham (2000) reported that individuals with extremely low scores on the L Scale have a higher education, more leadership responsibilities, and may be trying to exaggerate negative characteristics. The F or "Feeling bad/infrequency" Scale was designed to detect atypical responding. As F Scale scores increase, the assessee is indicating more unusual personal aspects. Those with very high scores may be highly unconventional individuals or may be attempting to exaggerate abnormality. Lees-Haley (1991), in a study of personal injury malingerers, found that the F Scale scores alone successfully classified 81 per cent of malingerers and 100 per cent of non-malingerers. The K or "Correction" Scale was designed as a subtle indicator of defensiveness, with low scores reflecting either true psychopathology or attempts to appear to be suffering psychopathological symptoms. It is only when viewed at a composite or overall profile that L, F, and K scale scores can be interpreted as pointing to deception (Greene, 1997).

While forensic cases of defensiveness only appear irregularly – in my experience, defensiveness is very rare and is usually the result of early and very traumatic experiences with mental health services – forensic cases of malingering are common (Rogers *et al.*, 2003). The social costs, at the very least, are greater when clients attempt to fake symptoms and disorders. A problem occurs, however, if the meaning of malingering is confounded, and I suspect that it may be within the MMPI-2. Sewell and Saleron (1997) suggested that detection of deception, especially malingering, proceed with caution with clients who have committed sexual offenses. Sexual offenders are unique offenders in many ways. In particular, they are different insofar as they must understand and explain their own anomalous behaviour (Horley, 2003a). This may present serious challenges in some cases. The middle-aged, active heterosexual father of two young children who has sexual contact with a prepubescent male is one such example. While engaged in forensic assessment and therapeutic activities over the years, I have certainly met a number of individuals who I believe were quite sincere in describing their utter mystification at their own behaviour. On occasion, I have asked such individuals to complete an MMPI-2, usually because of questions about possible deception. Some results have been "textbook examples", at least according to Butcher's (1990) text, of malingering. I have asked myself in some cases, however, where "malingerers" possessed very limited intellectual capacity and/or extreme thought disorder, whether there are alternative interpretations of MMPI-2 malingering. Might there be confounding of constructs that might, for example, deny a distinction between extremely confused and deception profiles? Helmes and Reddon (1993) pointed to a number of construct deficiencies in the MMPI-2. They noted, for example, that the meanings of some antiquarian terms, holdovers from the early days of the technique in the 1930s (Hathaway and McKinley, 1943), are unclear. My concern is that some offenders, and some sexual offenders in particular, may be viewed as "deceivers" or "malingerers" – a rather small step away from "liar" and "psychopath" – when in fact their personally baffling, impulsive, offensive behaviour produces a variety of attempts to understand themselves by "sampling" chaotic or alternative constructions or identities that may be translated in psychometric assessments like the MMPI-2 as attempts at deception. What appears required to understand in detail the meaning of malingering according to the MMPI-2 is a detailed analysis of the exact procedures, especially specific instructions to the original research participants, that led to the development of the validity scales.

Pascal's MMPI results revealed a variety of elevated substantive scales including schizophrenia, paranoia, social introversion, and psychopathic deviance. At the same time, all three main validity scales were either very high or low (viz., L and F were elevated while K was low). Such a pattern of results made the MMPI profile uninterpretable, but for me there were a couple of noteworthy findings. I frequently saw elevated paranoia and schizophrenia scales in assessments with offenders attempting to transfer from corrections to the mental health system, with paranoid schizophrenia undoubtedly construed as a probable ticket to a hospital for immediate treatment. In this case, two very "odd" scales, at least in terms of my experience, were elevated. Social introversion, referring to interpersonal withdrawal, and psychopathic deviance, referring to antisocial tendencies, tend to be rarely endorsed by dissembling offenders, probably because the resulting "antisocial loner" impression is not very flattering and unlikely to lead to a hospital admission. In Pascal's case, he did not seem to be particularly concerned about either going to a psychiatric facility or being viewed as an antisocial loner which, to some extent, was descriptive of his preincarceration lifestyle. These results seemed odd, and I was interested in exploring them further. After Pascal's unsuccessful attempt at early release, however, I was not sure that he would follow through with his stated interest in individual psychotherapy. Surprisingly, and thankfully, he did contact me after his parole hearing and requested to see me for treatment.

Cognitive restructuring with Pascal

Pascal had only two months of his two-year sentence remaining when we began weekly individual sessions because of the time he spent at the treatment centre. His last two months in our facility did not progress smoothly. Since his admission to maximum security, he had had occasional confrontations with both staff and inmates and, although these encounters did not result in serious assaults, probably due to Pascal's size and assumed physical ability, they did mean that he had few if any supporters. These confrontations increased in frequency, but not severity, as time went on. One of the supervisors of the shop where he worked for his entire stay in the institution described him as "a big kid . . . [who] threw temper tantrums" when given an order or request that he disagreed with. In the shop, his tantrums consisted of putting down his equipment, refusing to work, and glaring at whoever offended him. The supervisors tolerated a few minutes of such behaviour, and more often than not Pascal would return to work, but if not they would have him removed after 10 or 15 minutes of non-compliance. Placed on report, he would spend the next day or so in his own cell or in a segregation cell. Pascal's tantrums increased, and he missed one of our sessions in segregation. Because one other session was missed due to a visit from his father, Pascal and I spent only six individual therapy sessions together.

According to Kelly (1955), assessment and understanding of an individual's personal constructs do not occur only through formal, psychological assessment procedures. Any interview, however unstructured, and even informal conversation will reveal significant personal constructs. Our 60- to 90-minute sessions, while not resulting in a wealth of information, did reveal some significant ways that Pascal made sense of his social world. I asked very early into our first session about suicidal ideation and previous suicide attempts. Pascal was reluctant to talk about his feelings. There was a significant pause after every question put to him, especially if the question involved personal feelings and emotional experience. I was never sure if the search for such memories simply took him longer than many people or whether he edited material before presenting it to me. He admitted that he was often depressed, but he did not actively consider suicide, ever. He described his two previous suicide attempts as "attention-grabbers" rather than serious attempts to end his life. One episode involved tying a sweater around his own neck and choking himself while arguing with a teacher. For him, an attention-grabber was a very dramatic event that would garner some concern and intervention from those around him. He believed that, for the most part, all of his foster caregivers were more interested in government subsidies for his care than in him, and at times he needed to get their attention. He also used attention-grabbers as a request for therapy from professionals when he "was losing it" and felt that he needed some help. Pascal appeared to think long and hard, again perhaps editing, when I asked if his rather odd sexual assaults were attention-grabbers. He acknowledged initially that they could be, although he repeated that, at the time, what he was engaged in did not appear coercive or unpleasant to him. He described many of his sexual assaults as "just wrestling gone too far" but, when presented with details of his public assaults, refused to comment further except to conclude that his sexual assaults must have been due to something different.

Perhaps related closely to attention-grabbing was another important construct, "believes in me–doesn't believe in me". Pascal would often, usually as an aside, comment on any significant figure in his life that he or she either did or did not believe in him. Belief in him seemed to refer to whether he was accepted unconditionally as who he was rather than who he should be. His grandmother and father, as far as I could tell, were the only two people who truly believed in him from his perspective. None of his father's girlfriends, with perhaps the exception of the current live-in girlfriend who Pascal did not know well, ever believed in him. None of his brothers and sisters ever believed in him. Even his girlfriend, a relationship that seemed to end on his incarceration, did not believe in him. I had to ask whether he felt that any of the many professionals he had dealt with over the years, and I mentioned the names of two social workers in particular, ever believed in him. After considering for a while, he simply shrugged. He certainly gave the impression in his own rather quiet and understated manner that he was a misunderstood, forgotten, and isolated individual. Given the circumstances of his life to date, it seemed like he had every reason to see himself and others in such a manner. In terms of self-referential constructs, he described himself as "alone", "lonely", "misunderstood", "sad", and "a handful". He denied that he was in any way antisocial or a threat to others when asked directly.

Pascal had a difficult time discussing his own sexual past and sexual experiences. After such a question, he would stare off into space and, sometimes after a minute or two of silence, would suddenly shake his head and look at me as if awakening from a nightmare. He would rarely describe the images or memories at those times. Once, he did relate that he had been molested by an older sister when young. The details were not clear for him, and it was a painful memory, but he stated that it made him question himself. His first sexual assault on a young boy also made him wonder if he was "queer" and, when asked about his conclusion, he reported that he "must have been a little queer" to do such a thing. Queer, for Pascal, did not refer so much to homo-sexuality but to any form of sexually anomolous behaviour. Although he refused to acknowledge that "wrestling" with teenaged girls was in any way queer, he did agree that ripping the clothes from a teenager in a public street was "kinda queer". Being queer did not appear to have completely negative connotations for Pascal – it was just who he had become, a part of his current identity.

This was one point that I addressed during two subsequent sessions. I thought it might be helpful if Pascal could reinterpret queer as different or unique as opposed to sexually anomolous. By drawing connections to important aspects of diversity and "being your own person", and how every-one is different and idiosyncratic in many ways, I tried to allow him to see how queerness might be a very positive quality. He accepted that unique is just fine, but queer is simply unacceptable to others and would cause prob-lems for him should anyone discover how queer he was. We then returned to issues of his sexuality because I wanted him to consider his sexual self-identity. Again, much of this discussion elicited little or limited input on his part, although I liked to think that he was at least more open to the prospect of further efforts on this front. With Pascal, as with many of my clients, I viewed much of what I could do with them individually and/or in groups as simple preparatory work for the real work that they needed to do on release. My success in this attempt with Pascal was difficult to gauge.

Two weeks before his scheduled release from prison, Pascal received what, for him, was devastating news. His father had informed him that he could not live with him and his new girlfriend. Pascal blamed the woman but, while he may have been correct that the woman was less than thrilled about the pros-pect of a repeat sex offender living under her roof, it appeared as if his father was succumbing to intense media and public pressure. Pascal's father now lived in a large urban area that had experienced several high-profile serial sexual assaults and murders, and the prospect of more sexual offenders, espe-cially perceived "serious" ones, was not sitting well with residents. Pascal, not very talkative at the best of times, spent the last two weeks in a self-imposed silence. He worked rarely, and spent most of his time alone in his cell or with his social worker attempting to patch together a new release plan. He did come to his sessions with me, but was very morose and non-responsive. He described being abandoned again, and this time by someone who believed in him, and at a time when he needed help the most. He had arranged to see a forensic psychologist, a specialist I had recommended, and everything had fallen into place for him, at least until this serious setback. I tried to inject a positive note, pointing out that perhaps this was for the best due to past difficulties living with his father and the temptations of many young people around him, but he was having none of it. For him, it was a complete disaster.

I expected our final session to be more consolation than consultation, and possibly crisis intervention, but he appeared in an upbeat mood. He had just been told by his social worker that his grandmother had agreed to take him in, and arrangements were being finalized for his release to live with her in her rural community for at least the years of his probation order. He was looking forward to the help that she could provide on "the old ways". Since she was a relatively recent European immigrant, he believed that she could instruct him on successful farming techniques. I suspected that he was excited to be going to live with a supporter who could provide unconditional acceptance and love, and also connect him with a past, both recent and extended, that he really knew little about. I was concerned about the reality of the situation that the woman, well into her sixties and living alone, may not have been really prepared for. Nonetheless, I was willing to support his decision with necessary supports outside the home situation in place. As Pascal talked excitedly about his prospects and his improved likelihood of success now, I had to admit that the positivity that I was hearing was preferable to the negativity that I often heard on release from many offenders who really had no reason for optimism. Whether Pascal's optimism was misplaced or unrealistic remained to be seen.

Pascal's case conclusion

Pascal presented as a walking conundrum, one who had befuddled assessors and clinicians for years. His disrupted and turbulent early life experiences no doubt contributed to a confused and perhaps diffuse sense of self, including a very unclear perspective on his own sexuality. Pascal's past dealings with officialdom from a very young age also likely led to a distrust of authorities, and it limited the personal information and observations that he was willing to share with anyone in authority. No doubt it limited the outcomes of all assessment and treatment efforts.

Although Pascal may have been suspicious of me and my motives, he did seem interested in self-discovery, at least in his own manner. He seemed to present and to describe himself as a misunderstood, confused, and isolated individual who needed people to assist him by accepting him. Our few therapy sessions likely accomplished little in the way of active reconstrual and restructuring, but it is possible that Pascal may have come to see that personal change is indeed possible (Epting et al., 2003).

As I discovered later, Pascal completed his probation period without further incident and, at last report, was still living with his grandmother. It is reassuring to think that, at least in some cases, a young man on a rather worrying trajectory towards more violent sexual offenses could be sorted out by the firm and caring hand of a loving family member. Whether this family support came in time given 20 years of upheaval and abuse is difficult to tell, but I think we have to recognize that sometimes one person or one event can have a powerful enough impact to change or to reverse a life course. For Pascal's sake, and for the sake of all potential victims of all genders who could be involved with this man, I hope that he found what he needed in the form of psychological reconstruction.

Chapter 7

Final considerations

> I struggle very hard everyday . . . to prove to the outside world that I am not the monster some people would like to think I am.
>
> (Z. A., individual living in the community after serving two prison sentences for sexual assault, personal communication)

The quote above was provided to me in a very detailed letter by a former client, a well-educated and erudite individual who struggled with post-incarceration life. For him – although he did not see himself as a monster, he did apply a number of less harsh pejoratives to himself – society was shackling him on release from prison with the harsh social restrictions placed on ex-offenders, especially sexual offenders, but what he objected to most were the harsh labels that the media and neighbours applied to him. He was likely correct that most saw him, a recidivist who had victimized prepubescent individuals, as a monster or extreme deviant, a creature to be shunned if not worse. The question is whether we should regard sexual offenders, even dangerous repeat offenders, as monsters.

Moving beyond the current conceptual morass Marshall (1996) has provided an important paper for clinicians who work with sexual offenders. In his article, based on a keynote address that he gave at an international conference on sexual abuse, Marshall argued that most of us, including many forensic clinicians, regard sexual offenders as monsters beyond redemption. There is, however, every reason to view such an individual as "everyman", more like "sexual normals" than unlike them. According to Marshall, his clients behave as a function of their past encounters with other people rather than any biological imperative or genetic predisposition. In other words, experience is key for offenders as it appears to be for all of us – and he provided the example of one of his clients, a man he called "Fred". Although I am sure that I know the identity of Fred from some forensic assessments that I conducted in a high-security prison, Fred could be any number of offenders I have met over the years. When their stories are told at times, it is amazing how similar their lives are to many people's lives, although sometimes it is surprising that they are not more flawed individuals than they are. Fred's story is illustrative, and I will continue as if he is indeed the same individual I met around the time that Marshall wrote about him.

Fred was born into a poor, working-class family and was raised by a single parent who was stretched undoubtedly beyond her limits, both financially and emotionally. Fred provided more trouble for her than her many other children, and he was assessed by a professional early in life as "retarded". What soon followed was a series of institutional placements and, according to Fred, serious and continuous abuse, including physical and sexual, at the hands of institutional staff and other inmates. When he became an adolescent, Fred moved from victim to victimizer and he began to molest young males. He was a fairly serious child predator as an adult. Just before I met him, Fred had molested and murdered a prepubescent male. He was captured and sentenced to life in prison. Although he had undergone years of treatment, Fred maintained a very active sexual interest in young boys. His plan to escape from this ongoing compulsion was to save himself and others by becoming a psychologist, a sex offender treatment specialist, in order to repay society for the harm he had done by helping those he could relate to most closely. I avoided any encouragement of such a plan, even silence, lest it be construed as support for his new direction in life.

Fred served his time in a maximum-secure penitentiary because of the notoriety of his case. He seemed to me oblivious to the cat-calls that rained down on him constantly, including many death threats. Once, after I asked whether he was worried about the insults and threats, he shrugged and passed them off as part of the "macho" posturing of prison life, especially because he viewed most of his critics as men who had committed far worse crimes than he had. He conducted himself in a nonchalant manner, not too surprising given his life spent largely within uncaring if not brutal institutions. Fred decided to work in the institutional tailor shop despite warnings, including a plea from me, against this course of action. He survived only a few days before another inmate stabbed him in the back and killed him. The cheers that I saw in the media and heard within the prison no doubt reflected the beliefs of many who viewed Fred as a monster who deserved death for his repeated, hideous offenses. The cheering, however, seemed to me to reflect badly on all of us, inmate and non-inmate alike. I had been offered a brief glimpse of a man, however flawed, who had been most probably the product of many horrendous experiences that we in society had inflicted upon him, either via commission or omission. True, it was impossible to know exactly which if any among his reported early life traumas actually occurred. Fred clearly had a vested interest in presenting himself as injured and aggrieved, but I have seen many individuals, some who all would agree were "young and innocent", abused within many different institutional settings. Some of the abuse was physical and some sexual, but much of it was emotional. Surprisingly for me, at least initially, much of the abuse was delivered by staff. In a sense, however, all members of a society are responsible when those in total institutions, whether hospitals or prisons, really any institution, are abused by caretakers.

The process of making monsters appears to be a longstanding and "functional" process. Monsters appear to exist for a reason. In general, they tend to serve as warnings about certain human activities, whether tinkering with technology or walking in the woods alone at night. Modern monsters appear very different from our earlier creations in that they are seldom loathsome in appearance, but this less-than-remarkable appearance is even more frightening in some ways. Not only do they look very much like us, but they are able to walk among us, even during daylight hours, and slip by nearly unnoticed except for very subtle warning signs. Sex offenders as monsters exist to warn all of us about the woes of sexuality gone to extremes. While the limits of acceptable sexual behaviour vary over time and culture – not too long ago in Western countries (see APA, 1968), a book like this would have included a serious discussion of gay and lesbian sex – sex offenders still provide tangible examples of what and who to avoid sexually. Unfortunately, as monsters, they frighten us so much that the only appropriate response seems to be their destruction, or at least long-term incapacitation in a secure institution. At this point, it appears to be time to think about sex offenders less as monsters and more as men, and in some cases women, in need of treatment, and the treatment that I have in mind is not execution, either direct by the state or indirect by fellow inmates, who were recently termed "moral inmates" by a Canadian politician suggesting that the best treatment for sexual offenders was to be sent into the general prison population.

The rehabilitation of sexual offenders, however, can present us with dilemnas. On the one hand, we are repulsed by their actions, angered by their brazen disregard for others, and want to punish them severely for the pain they have caused. On the other hand, we sympathize with at least a few of them, on occasion declaring them not guilty by reason of insanity, and want to provide some opportunity for improvement. There appears no reason why both accountability and rehabilitation can occur simultaneously for sexual offenders, and I believe that we should make more effort to offer all sexual offenders judicial dispositions that are more therapeutic. If we can think more clearly about the nature of these individuals and their offenses, changes can be made to accommodate offenders who are willing to consider alternatives to their unacceptable behaviours.

Our problems concerning the conceptualization of sexual offenders date from at least the nineteenth century. We may owe a debt of gratitude to clinician-investigators like Krafft-Ebing (1886/1965) for their documentation of the varieties of sexual variation and abuse, but their nosological work on offenders began a downward slide into simplistic categorization, if it was not simplistic to begin with. Continued refinement of existing categories (e.g., APA, 2000), with many terms borrowed from Krafft-Ebing and colleagues, appears to be pointless tinkering (Horley, 2001). Rather than more attractive Procrustean beds, or perhaps we should regard them as conceptual coffins, we should toss out the beds, all attempts at categorization, and aim for a more dimensional perspective with respect to sex abuse and sex offenders. If we need to use the term "diagnosis" with sex offenders, and I would prefer to avoid it altogether, the best way to describe it would be a dimensional or transitive diagnosis (Kelly, 1955). Adoption of a dimensional approach to sexual offending in general can be advantageous. If nothing else, use of even two dimensions, such as activity and age, might help place different types of offenders in the same "sexual space" as non-offenders to help illustrate the continuum, or continua, that exist with respect to sexual behaviour.

PCT is clearly not the only option in terms of a theoretical foundation for a new approach to dealing with sexual offenders – as various writers have suggested previously (e.g., Marshall and Barbaree, 1990; Marshall, 1996; Horley, 2000), cognitive social learning theory (Bandura, 1977, 1986) can serve as a good basis for such an approach – although I would argue that many of the alternatives, especially cognitive social learning theory, are subsumed by PCT. Whatever the choice, we do need to embrace change. Avoidance of all categorical thinking and analyses, the basis of essentialism and static views of people, appears to be key. The legal implication of declaring an individual mentally ill yet responsible for their actions, while certainly not unheard of in all jurisdictions, is problematic. It is a problem that may be exceeded by the personal paradox of viewing yourself, as a convicted sex offender, as both responsible yet not responsible for your actions. "My biology/genetics made me do it!" is no more satisfactory an answer to the question of the origins of sexual assault than saying "My family made me do it!" or "The devil made me do it!" We are, at some level, responsible for our choices, and the notion of will, largely lost in psychology throughout the twentieth century, should be invoked.

Our choices to harm can be countered by our choices to heal. We need to accept that anyone can, if willing and if provided with realistic alternatives, choose to address personal deficits that promote self-harm and hurt other people. If we continue to tell our clients, however unintentionally, that they are engaged in offensive sexual behaviour because that is who they really are in terms of genetics, pathological personality traits, biochemistry, or any constitutional factor, they are unlikely to attempt to change. What would be the point of attempting to fight against nature? All too often I have heard offenders, including my clients, conclude, "Fuck it! I am who I am! I might as well accept myself and do what I do best." Such a conclusion is often the result of frustration and disappointment, sometimes simply a passing expression of exasperation. While I may not agree, and certainly argue against such a fatalistic acceptance of the pronouncements of others, I can see how they might come to such a conclusion. The message is out there, not only in the media and public but among forensic mental health professionals, that sexual offenders are born with pathological traits or other characteristics that account for their offensive sexual behaviour. Besides, if you have been engaged in anomolous and harmful sexual behaviour for many years – indeed, any form of sexual involvement – the effort required to change under any circumstances is serious. It is much easier to accept the devil known than the one unknown.

We benefit no one, unless it is ourselves and our own predictions of failure on the part of repeat offenders, if we label others as defective or pathological congenitally. We need to keep in mind, too, that we provide little if any hope of improvement if we only offer a symptom management option. Daily or monthly medication is not a very satisfying possibility if you believe that, except for the pill or injection, you would revert to the sexual monster that is the real you. For true hope of improvement to be offered to our clients who have committed sexual offenses, we need to present the possibility, without making the outcome an inevitability, that they can indeed change from a person who would readily hurt people into a person who would have a great deal of difficulty hurting others. The required message is that the real root of the problem is traceable and can be eliminated.

If we do embrace a psychological theory like PCT, it needs to be sufficiently comprehensive to include all aspects of sexual abuse within its focus of convenience. Presently, PCT is not sufficiently developed in that it does not include a sophisticated analysis of the social world and social psychology. Why this is the case is open to speculation. As Neimeyer (1985) made very clear, much of the energy of PCT researchers and clinicians over the first three decades of the theory was devoted to rep grid research and specific areas of inquiry, such as research into thought disorder. Relatively little attention was devoted to theoretical elaboration, and the results of the neglect are now being felt. The social psychological implications of PCT must be examined and developed, and it appears insufficient to note that PCT contains a sociality corollary describing the importance of social roles. The nature of elements and, in particular, the nature of social interaction are just two broad areas that I see as central for examination.

Social power, largely ignored within PCT, does appear to have a place in the theory. Power does not just refer to particular constructs, but it refers primarily to a relational characteristic that is based on social elemental strengths. Although sexual offenders, especially successful ones, may be skilled in the arts of wielding power and controlling victims, they are not necessarily using power for the sake of power. Power, as a relational characteristic, tends to be a means to an end rather than an end in itself. Power, as a construct, however, can be an end in itself. A successful assault that validates a core construct like "powerful–weak", with powerful applied to the self, undoubtedly supplies exhilaration and increases the likelihood of reoffense. It is not likely, however, that the rape or abuse of another sexually would validate one such construct. If nothing else, PCT research has demonstrated that complexity of a person's construct system is the rule rather than the exception. The hundreds of thousands of personal constructs that comprise any individual's system, and the hierarchical and other complex relations among those constructs, make it unlikely that a single construct accounts for any behaviour. Any expression of human sexuality probably involves many different interrelated constructs, and it validates and/or invalidates any number of constructs simultaneously. The difficult task of sorting out this complexity falls to forensic mental health professionals, at least those interested and willing to forego the simplicity of categorical assessment of sexual offenders, and we need to get on with the job rather than looking for simple answers. There is no reason why sexual assault must involve either power or sexuality as primary "motives". A more nuanced view would acknowledge that, probably for many abusers, both play a role in their sexual offenses, perhaps simultaneously.

Personal constructs of sexual offenders

While it would be encouraging to state definitively how sexual offenders, or perhaps subtypes of offenders, construe themselves and their victims, this cannot be done. Many factors can be cited as responsible for this state of affairs. Not only is this research endeavour mere years into organized inquiry but, because it is not a mainstream view within psychology or psychiatry, it lacks the funding and other resources to advance. The work done to date is intriguing but very preliminary.

Most of the research on the constructs or cognitions of sexual offenders, both within PCT and in psychology generally, has focussed on men who become involved sexually with children. Although we might discover some common constructions among all child molesters, this appears unlikely given the heterogeneity of these offenders. It may well be that dominance and submission represent an important construct for many child molesters, where children are interpreted as submissive and non-threatening while adults are viewed as dominant and imposing. Such a finding may, too, be related to the self-construal of child molesters as less attractive sexually. This requires further study, however, and there are indications that only men who become involved with young girls might think in such terms. Men who are very violent and prey on young children (i.e., child rape-murderers, those in the extreme upper left quadrant of the two-dimensional age-activity graph) may construe men, especially themselves, as cruel and attractive. This possibility, however, is very preliminary and based on a very few individuals among a thankfully small population.

Men who engage in sexual coercion with adults have been less well studied. It is possible that some rapists engage in extremely simplistic views of women as either "pure" or "dirty", perhaps reflecting a cognitive simplicity or tight construction. Preliminary study, however, indicates that it does not appear to be a common construction, at least among those men who are non-violent. Men who assault women have been found to have views supportive of the rape myths, and this may increase a likelihood of using force during a sexual encounter, especially when accompanied by a sense of hostility toward women. It really is very premature to conclude anything about rapists' constructions.

So-called "nuisance" offenders, such as men who exhibit their genitalia in public or who engage in public voyeurism, may be common and have many victims, but they are also a very disparate and varied group. They appear to have a broad range of possible constructions and reasons for their sexually anomalous behaviour. There is very little chance of finding any common constructions among these offenders unless it is a very general finding concerning a self-perception as, for example, "perverse" or "different".

The question concerning the structure and content of sexual offenders' personal construct systems may be very open at present, but answers will come as further research is conducted. While constructs common to subtypes of sex offenders (e.g., those who molest only prepubescent males) might be discovered, the successful research will likely focus on the individual level. No doubt research into developing and improving existing assessment techniques will improve our understanding of offenders' construction processes. The issue of improved treatment options for sex offenders to lower their likelihood of reoffense is an important one, and it too is tied to the larger research question.

A new emphasis in assessment for sexual offenders may be on the horizon. Old "standards", like penile plethysmography, while still in use, appear to be losing favour for a number of very valid reasons (Marshall, 2006). Popular psychometric measures, too, may be continuing but at a diminishing rate. Such a decrease is no doubt justified because of the relatively poor predictive performance of such measures in general forensic use (Gendreau, 2002), or because the findings with respect to sex offenders are inconsistent (cf., McCreary, 1975; Lanyon, 1986). It seems to me that some idiographic techniques, like the rep grid, may fill the void left by diminished use of the old standard assessments. Although the rep grid has never been a wildly popular technique in forensic assessment, probably due in large part to the time and effort required for the analysis, it does appear to be a sensitive device for assessing therapeutic change in forensic settings. Other very simple idiographic assessments have been used, and they could certainly be employed more extensively, but new techniques could be developed. A self-characterization sketch (Kelly, 1955) can be used effectively in various assessment and therapeutic situations. Even asking a related question such as "Who are you?" in a therapy session can provide useful personal information. The resulting data, perhaps too abundant to an assessor used to scoring objective tests quickly and having a normative profile drop from a machine, can provide a rich source of information about a client who would otherwise remain a puzzle. If we view the psychological assessment procedure as the process by which valid psychological predicates are ascribed to individuals, the means by which those predicates are arrived at should not necessarily be limited to a few "pet" techniques or even a single approach. Exploration of new techniques and procedures is of the utmost importance when it comes to client groups like sexual offenders. Overcoming a reluctance to delve into personal difficulties is required of any useful assessment, and innovative assessments might consider other ways of accomplishing this not so easy feat.

A major limitation of almost all of the research done to date with sexual offenders, within PCT and beyond, concerns an inherent bias that probably affects our views of offenders. Most of the research has included only incarcerated offenders. Not only might we be examining highly specific characteristics or subtypes of sex offender (e.g., more violent, desires capture and punishment, less intelligent), but the processes of adjudication and incarceration can have a profound impact on various psychological aspects of the offenders, probably the very variables we are concerned with. Arrest by the police, especially in a high-profile case with its mandatory "perp walk", is likely traumatizing enough for some individuals. When combined with a long and very public trial, the experience must have a profound effect on almost everyone at the centre of it. Combined with years of imprisonment in what, even for the most entitled of inmates which sex offenders definitely are not, can best be described as brutal and inhumane warehouses, there is no doubt that an offender's self-image and self-esteem, as well as views of people in general, will be altered seriously.

Researchers like Wilson and Cox (1983a, 1983b) deserve kudos for their attempt to recruit a sample of non-adjudicated, non-incarcerated sexual offenders, but the likelihood of a very generalizable sample coming from an organization that calls itself the "Paedophile Information Exchange" is very low, unless we are only interested in the political, the predatory, the reckless, the compulsive, etc. among men who abuse children sexually. To obtain samples of men who are non-adjudicated and non-incarcerated is unbelievably challenging on a number of fronts. Even if an advertisement succeeded in attracting the attention and interest of a number of appropriate volunteers in the community, unquestionably the police and courts would be very keen, understandably so, to see the participant recruitment list. Over a number of years, I have seen only two individuals who had not been referred by the courts or prison service. The non-adjudicated men who approached me for assistance did so very reluctantly and skittishly, and they quickly terminated treatment, the longest lasting six weeks. The fear of detection, regardless of assurances of anonymity from both an individual therapist and a public institution, was too great to commit to any prolonged and, possibly, helpful involvement in therapy. We need to decide collectively whether the importance of public trial and punishment outweighs the importance of addressing personal problems that have led, or may lead, to the abuse of others.

Improving psychotherapeutic services for sexual offenders

Clearly, more theoretical and empirical investigation of sexual offenders is required in order to improve psychotherapeutic service. Further study will clarify what treatment works with what client group with which clinicians and where. There are many issues, however, that need to be considered when addressing the issue of improved services for sexual offenders.

One important overriding issue concerns the setting of service delivery for sexual offender programming. A number of writers (e.g., Milan *et al.*, 1999; Horley and Bennett, 2003; Schneider, *et al.*, 2006) have discussed some of the general problems with implementing and maintaining programs for any offenders, as well as specific problems when dealing with difficult clients like sexual offenders, in essentially non-therapeutic settings like prisons. I cannot count the number of times incarcerated clients have remarked on how little correction actually occurs within correctional facilities. While some of the difficulty lies with the nature of the physical plants of prisons (e.g., built for security) or the setting, perhaps the more serious obstacles to effective correctional programming lie in the atmosphere or attitudes of the people in the places, the set. Correctional staff can present serious treatment obstacles to therapeutic improvement by openly displaying non-conducive views of change (e.g., sex offenders are unable to change, therapists are charlatans). I have witnessed months of therapeutic improvement vanish in an instant on a prison range after a well-timed, well-phrased public comment by a staff member.

A deeper and more subtle problem appears to exist in many if not all prisons. The mindset that appears necessary for survival in the vicious world of most prisons is not very conducive to therapeutic insight and change. Incarcerated offenders tend to divide their social worlds into prosocial (i.e., "Them" or the authorities) versus antisocial (i.e., "Us" or the inmates) aspects (see Horley, 2005b, for more details). Such preemptive construal, where a person can become "solid-and-nothing-but-solid", is extremely adaptive insofar as unequivocal and quick responses tend to follow (e.g., assault, abrupt aversion of gaze). Hesitation behind prison walls is weakness, and the weak are construed as prey who may not survive. Many of my incarcerated clients have learned, some due to decades of incarceration, that the most adaptive approach psychologically to incarceration is to view everyone as either "like you" or "not like you". This places all prison-based therapists in the awkward position of being seen as the enemy or, at the very least, someone not easily trusted. This lack of trust by many incarcerated clients may be justified to a large extent in that many forensic therapists are insensitive to the daily lives of their clients. By asking them to adopt more prosocial alternatives, we may well lessen chances of survival in prison by making an offender client appear weak to incarcerated associates. This is a very problematic situation not easily overcome given current practices and conditions.

One consideration that might help both therapist and client would be to humanize working conditions by establishing more "treatment centre" approaches. The suggestion made by several writers (see Cabeen and Coleman, 1961; Cullen *et al.*, 1997) of providing a therapeutic community (Roberts, 1997) for offenders, even within prison walls, is a good example of how we might proceed. The stark reality of most prisons, even the newest and most "progressive", is that they are brutal micro-environments for some of the most egregious examples of inhumanity. What would serve to "soften" the treatment environment would be to separate all treatment programs, whether for sex offenders or others, and literally move them, not to some other part of the prison ground within the perimeter wall or fence, but to some other site entirely. Only by doing so could the culture of violence and the pressure that comes from the daily struggle for survival, both physical and emotional, that is life in many prisons be breached.

By making such a physical change, a second change would likely be facilitated. The mental health of forensic clinicians, who work with some of the most difficult clients imaginable, needs to be taken more seriously. Steps are required to protect clinicians from "burn-out" and other work-related problems (Schneider *et al.*, 2006). Even untrained undergraduates who meet frontline workers can notice and regularly do remark on the ravages of the job conditions. More sabbaticals, work leaves, or job swapping/sharing might provide the breaks for difficult work that is absolutely necessary for these workers.

Attracting more clinicians into this area is a vital consideration. Few clinicians, even forensic ones, choose to work with sexual offenders. Whether this is due to personal repugnance over their actions, the thankless nature of the work, or some other personal or professional concern is difficult to determine. Certainly the prospect of working in correctional facilities is not an attractive possibility for many clinicians, new or established. In the forensic courses that I teach, especially advanced clinical ones, I will often find a dozen or more bright, young, energetic would-be clinicians ready not only to work with offenders but keen to work with sex offenders in particular. After a term or two of discussion about sexual abuse, and visits to prisons and forensic hospitals to meet the offenders and frontline staff, the number is reduced usually to one or two "maybes" in terms of work with sex offenders. It is not that the courses have been so painful in general that they have lost an interest in the field because the courses are highly rated and the students generally tell me that the experiences have been great. They claim, however, that they have simply "moved on" and are looking for a client group more suited to what they have to offer. In other words, they really do not feel that, given existing situations in many institutional and community settings where sex offenders are treated, they could have much impact. Sometimes the discussion turns to changes in the workplace to make it more attractive to clinicians, and there are a number of points that I have heard. One issue that has arisen concerns the ability of treatment staff to design and implement sound programs. Many students, especially the brightest and most creative, are unimpressed by the makeshift programming, if any, that is available in many forensic work-places. The bureaucracy that they encounter, usually dominated by very conservative security specialists, produces pessimism about the chances for improvements. If we are identifying and designing more effective program-ming, we should allow the wide-scale development and expansion of existing services. Related to the issue of research, many new clinicians would, I believe, find forensic settings more attractive if there were more in-house research opportunities available. If we were to make more funding available for program evaluation, and not just "institutional bean-counting" evalu-ations but using more and better outcome measures of interest to those beyond the narrow ministry or organization, we could attract and keep the very scientist-practitioners that we prize so highly in the academy.

An important avenue of further psychotherapeutic practice and research concerns multifaceted or multimodal programs. A multimodal approach to treatment programming has been advocated not only within psycho-therapeutic circles broadly (e.g., Lazarus, 1971) but within the treatment of offenders narrowly (e.g., Quinsey, 1977; Marshall and Barbaree, 1988). Such an approach does not rely on a single treatment modality but advocates a range of different treatments within a single theoretically integrated program. Multimodal programming appears particularly germane to sex offenders because even groupings of sexual offenders (e.g., men who molest prepubes-cent individuals) should not be construed as homogeneous and requiring a single form of intervention. Unfortunately, all sex offenders are frequently stereotyped as a homogeneous group. A problem with the literature on both violent offenders and sexual offenders is the tendency to view them as having common constructions. Given that Prentky and Knight (1991) and others have demonstrated that there are many different subtypes of rapists and child molesters, while Winter (2003a) has argued convincingly that there are many constructivistic roots to violence, there is no reason to view all sexual offenders as sharing very much of any psychological characteristic. The more I have worked with sex offenders, in fact all offenders, the more I am con-vinced that individual analysis, followed perhaps by some level of aggrega-tion, is the only way to proceed. Offering a variety of different types of psychotherapy can assist clients in addressing a range of personal problems, and it is clear that many factors can influence a difficulty like, for example, public displays of genitalia. Many of my clients have been involved in drug and alcohol rehabilitation, life skills training, and a heterosocial skills group in addition to one or more components of my program. Although treatment resources are scarce, and this seems to be especially true in forensic settings in most jurisdictions, it appears to be worthwhile to scramble for the resources to provide a range or choice of services to clients who have committed sex offences. Naturally, expanded opportunity for forensic clinicians, constructivistic and otherwise, is an important component in providing choice in terms of sex offender treatment.

Much more research is required on treatment efficacy. The important work by Viney *et al.* (2005) demonstrating the effectiveness of many forms of personal construct psychotherapy is encouraging, but more work needs to be done in the area of forensic personal construct psychotherapy (Horley, 2005b). When it comes to implementing programs, community-based programs seem to be the most effective in terms of setting (Andrews and Bonta, 1998). Community settings appear preferable for a number of reasons (Gendreau, 1996), even with or especially with clients like sexual offenders (see Eccles and Walker, 2003). Community psychology has challenged forensic clinicians to provide services in a more efficient manner (see Roesch, 1988). Perhaps even the setting proposed by community psychology, the local community, should be considered more from a forensic treatment perspective. While I am not aware of any PCT-inspired, community-based forensic programs, they are clearly necessary.

I think we as forensic clinicians need to focus on techniques and therapeutic approaches that build on the existing strengths of our offender clients. With respect to clients who have committed sexual offenses, this is an important area that is largely ignored (Horley, 2005a, 2006), although very recently there are signs that this deficit is being addressed by sex offender treatment specialists. Ward and colleagues (e.g., Ward and Gannon, 2006) are promoting what they call a "Good Lives Model" for sex offender therapy. They do not support simply targetting intrapersonal and interpersonal deficits in their clients, but they argue that sexual offenders need support and guidance in constructing more adaptive self-identities. They would have us approach this enterprise by more concern with identifying offenders' personal values, or primary goods, and working with them to develop new and more successful behaviours to achieve these abstract ends or principles. This is very similar to a PCT perspective on reconstruing the self and others. True, the gist of PCT is change in values or core constructs, but there is nothing wrong with finding new and successful behavioural experiments in line with existing constructs that do not involve harming others. Building on client strengths while at the same time addressing weaknesses, the problematic constructs or ways of construing oneself and other individuals, appears to be the most effective strategy for assisting offenders.

Marshall (1996) has provided a good overall strategy for forensic clinicians to proceed with in terms of work with sex offender clients. He recommended that we need "to display respect for our clients, help them distinguish their offensive behaviors from themselves, display compassion and empathy, model egalitarian attitudes, and, most of all, convey a belief in the redeemable nature of all people, including sexual offenders" (p. 332). This last point indicates hope for change. Hope appears to be an important aspect in successful psychotherapy (see Farran *et al.*, 1995), a factor that has been examined for a number of years (Frank, 1968). Hope, unfortunately, is in short supply among most sexual offenders I have seen, and we as forensic clinicians need to convey to our clients hope for improvement if significant effort is expended. What I have in mind here, to be clear, is not the false hope of quick and painless improvement, but the hope that improvement and change are possible. Most often, clinical students when first confronting the possibility of providing clinical services to sex offenders wonder about wasted efforts because they, probably like most laypeople, see sex offenders as incorrigible. Change in this position is accomplished upon presentation of contrary evidence, such as the finding that the index/sexual recidivism rate for sexual offenders is typically 10–15 per cent over a period of five years at risk in the community (Hanson and Morton-Bourgon, 2005). However we accomplish it, we need to convince all involved that sexual offenders can alter their "wicked ways". This idea of promoting hope of change with sex offenders has been discussed recently by Moulton and Marshall (2005). Unfortunately, their suggestions are limited by their use of psychodiagnostics and psychiatric labels (Marshall, 2006). For true hope for change to be instilled in our sex offender clients, we need to abandon all psychiatric nosologies and related terminology, otherwise they will recognize the contradiction that they are presented with and they will, at some point, likely abandon whatever hope they may have. Hope, like empathy and many of the other treatment targets we have or may have with our clients, is difficult to acquire and very easy to lose.

As I look back over more than 20 years of research and treatment with sexual offenders, I can say that I know some individual sexual offenders well, although I cannot say that I know sexual offenders well as a group. Probably by employing a credulous approach, and actually trying to understand what my clients were trying to tell me, I have gained insights into a few individuals' inner lives. Although I am concerned about not understanding the group better, I am not overly worried. Given the range and diversity of behaviour viewed as sexual offending, the group designation of "sexual offender" is a broad one at best, and perhaps more legalistic than psychological. At this point in time, I would argue that understanding and assisting single individuals, even if within a group format, is an admirable target. If we can devise community-based, preventative programs aimed at potential abusers sometime in the future, so much the better, but the principles of such programming might well be based on the findings of clinical research with single offenders.

However much we might want to punish sexual offenders, we must recognize that rehabilitation trumps punishment. At any rate, rehabilitation of sexual offenders is not coddling them. I have heard the remark often from incarcerated offenders, particularly sexual offenders, that treatment programming is among the most difficult time spent behind bars. We have taken their freedom on incarceration, and we can keep them behind bars for longer periods should they show no interest in altering harmful patterns of behaviour. It is not humane, and frankly not fair, that we condemn them to a lifetime of marginal existence, if not continued sanction, by simply supplying offenders with a label, or several. Whether the label is pedophile or psychopath, it carries stigma and, more importantly, the ability to produce a long-term offender, assuming one has already not been created by the internalization of prior labels. Social labelling is a process that we can control, and we must control it if we are to address the problems of crime and criminal victimization. The situation of addressing sexual abuse is not as simple as ceasing the categorization of abusers by clinicians, but this would be a good step in combination with other steps. Soon, we will be running toward a solution to this major social problem. A serious point to keep in mind when considering the overall social costs of sex offender treatment expansion is the continued, escalating costs of doing nothing or too little. As Prentky and Burgess (1990) have documented, the financial cost to the criminal justice system of addressing sexual offenses is enormous. We need to make some difficult decisions with respect to sexual offenders, and the time to do that is now.

References

Abel, G. G., and Blanchard, E. B. (1974). The role of fantasy in the treatment of sexual deviation. *Archives of General Psychiatry*, *30*, 467–475.

Abel, G. G., Becker, J. V., and Cunningham-Rathner, J. (1984). Complications, consent, and cognitions in sex between children and adults. *International Journal of Law and Psychiatry*, *7*, 89–103.

Abel, G. G., Becker, J. V., Cunningham-Rathner, J., Mittelman, M., and Rouleau, J. (1988). Multiple paraphilic diagnoses among sex offenders. *Bulletin of the American Academy of Psychiatry and the Law*, *16*, 153–168.

Adams, H. E., and McAnulty, R. D. (1993). Sexual disorders: The paraphilias. In H. E. Adams and P. B. Sutker (Eds.), *Comprehensive handbook of psychopathology* (pp. 563–579). New York: Plenum Press.

Adams-Webber, J. R. (1970a). An analysis of the discriminant validity of several repertory grid indices. *British Journal of Psychology*, *61*, 83–90.

Adams-Webber, J. R. (1970b). Elicited versus provided constructs in repertory grid technique: A review. *British Journal of Medical Psychology*, *43*, 349–354.

Adams-Webber, J. R. (1979). *Personal construct theory: Concepts and applications*. New York: Wiley.

Adams-Webber, J. R. (1989). Some reflections on the "meaning" of repertory grid responses. *International Journal of Personal Construct Psychology*, *6*, 77–92.

Adams-Webber, J. R., and Davidson, D. (1979). Maximum contrast between self and others in personal judgement: A repertory grid study. *British Journal of Psychology*, *70*, 517–518.

Adams-Webber, J., and Neff, G. (1996). Developmental trends and gender differences in construing self and parents. *Journal of Constructivist Psychology*, *9*, 225–232.

Adams-Webber, J. R., and Rodney, Y. (1983). Rational aspects of temporary changes in construing self and others. *Canadian Journal of Behavioural Sciences*, *15*, 52–59.

American Psychiatric Association (1952). *Diagnostic and statistical manual of mental disorders*. Washington: American Psychiatric Association.

American Psychiatric Association (1968). *Diagnostic and statistical manual* (2nd ed.). Washington: American Psychiatric Association.

American Psychiatric Association (1980). *Diagnostic and statistical manual* (3rd ed.). Washington: American Psychiatric Association.

American Psychiatric Association (1994). *Diagnostic and statistical manual* (4th ed.). Washington: American Psychiatric Association.

American Psychiatric Association (2000). *Diagnostic and statistical manual – text revision* (4th ed.). Washington: American Psychiatric Association.

Andrews, D. A., and Bonta, J. (1998). *The psychology of criminal conduct*. Cincinatti: Anderson.

Andrews, D. A., and Wormith, J. S. (1990). *A summary of normative, reliability, and validity statistics on the Criminal Sentiments Scale*. Unpublished manuscript, Carleton University, Ottawa.

Andrews, D. A., Zinger, I., Hoge, R., Bonta, J., Gendreau, P., and Cullen, F. T. (1990). Does correctional treatment work? A clinically relevant and psychologically informed meta-analysis. *Criminology, 28*, 369–404.

Badesha, J., and Horley, J. (2000). Self-construal among psychiatric outpatients. *British Journal of Medical Psychology, 73*, 547–551.

Bandura, A. (1971). Psychotherapy based upon modeling principles. In A. E. Bergin and S. L. Garfield (Eds.), *Handbook of psychotherapy and behavior change: An empirical analysis* (pp. 241–279). New York: Wiley.

Bandura, A. (1982). Self-efficacy mechanism in personal agency. *American Psychologist, 37*, 122–147.

Bandura, A. (1986). *Social foundations in thought and action: A social cognitive theory*. Englewood Cliffs: Prentice-Hall.

Bannister, D. (1965). The rationale and clinical relevance of repertory grid technique. *British Journal of Psychiatry, 111*, 977–982.

Bannister, D. (Ed.) (1970). *Perspectives in personal construct theory*. London: Academic Press.

Bannister, D. (1972). Critiques of the concept of "loose construing": A reply. *British Journal of Social and Clinical Psychology, 11*, 412–414.

Bannister, D. (1973). Reply to Haynes and Phillips. *British Journal of Social and Clinical Psychology, 12*, 324–325.

Bannister, D. (1979). Personal construct theory and politics. In P. Stringer and D. Bannister (Eds.), *Constructs of sociality and individuality* (pp. 21–34). London: Academic Press.

Bannister, D., and Agnew, J. (1977). The child's construing of self. In J. K. Cole and A. W. Landfield (Eds.), *Nebraska symposium on motivation* (Vol. 24, pp. 99–125). Lincoln: University of Nebraska.

Bannister, D., and Fransella, F. (1966). A grid test of schizophrenic thought disorder. *British Journal of Social and Clinical Psychology, 5*, 95–102.

Bannister, D., and Fransella, F. (1971). *Inquiring man: The theory of personal constructs*. Harmondsworth: Penguin.

Bannister, D., and Mair, J. M. M. (1968). *The evaluation of personal constructs*. London: Academic Press.

Bannister, D., Fransella, F., and Agnew, J. (1971). Characteristics and validity of the grid test of thought disorder. *British Journal of Social and Clinical Psychology, 10*, 144–151.

Bannister, D., Adams-Webber, J. R., Penn, W. I., and Radley, A. R. (1975). Reversing the process of thought disorder: A serial validation experiment. *British Journal of Social and Clinical Psychology, 14*, 169–180.

Barbaree, H. (1989). *Denial and minimization among adolescent and adult sexual offenders*. Paper presented at the Conference on the Adolescent Sexual Offender, Vancouver, Canada, November.

Barbaree, H. E., Seto, M. C., Langton, C. M., and Peacock, E. J. (2001). Evaluating the predictive accuracy of six risk assessment instruments for adult sex offenders. *Criminal Justice and Behavior, 28*, 490–521.

Bavelas, J. B., Chan, A. S., and Guthrie, J. A. (1976). Reliability and validity of traits measured by Kelly's Repertory Grid. *Canadian Journal of Behavioural Science, 8*, 23–38.

Bell, A. P., and Hall, C. S. (1971). *The personality of a child molester: An analysis of dreams*. Chicago: Aldine.

Benjafield, J., and Adams-Webber, J. R. (1975). Assimilative projection and construct balance in the repertory grid. *British Journal of Psychology, 66*, 169–173.

Berliner, L. (1991). Clinical work with sexually abused children. In C. R. Hollin and K. Howells (Eds.), *Clinical approaches to sex offenders and their victims* (pp. 209–228). New York: Wiley.

Bieri, J. (1955). Cognitive complexity–simplicity and predictive behavior. *Journal of Abnormal and Social Psychology, 51*, 263–268.

Bonarius, J. C. J. (1965). Research in the personal construct theory of George A. Kelly. In B. Maher (Ed.), *Progress in experimental personality research* (Vol. 2, pp. 1–46). New York: Academic Press.

Bonarius, J. C. J. (1970). Fixed role therapy: A double paradox. *British Journal of Medical Psychology, 43*, 213–219.

Bradford, J. M. W. (1990). The antiandrogen and hormonal treatment of sex offenders. In W. L. Marshall, D. R. Laws, and H. E. Barbaree (Eds.), *Handbook of sexual assault* (pp. 297–310). New York: Plenum Press.

Brownmiller, S. (1975). *Against our will: Men, women, and rape*. New York: Simon and Schuster.

Bumby, K. M. (1996). Assessing the cognitive distortions of child molesters and rapists: Development and validation of the RAPE and MOLEST scales. *Sexual Abuse: A Journal of Research and Treatment, 8*, 37–54.

Burkitt, I. (1996). Social and personal constructs: A division left unresolved. *Theory and Psychology, 6*, 71–77.

Buss, D. M. (1994). *The evolution of desire: Strategies of human mating*. New York: Basic Books.

Butcher, J. N. (1990). *MMPI-2 in psychological treatment*. New York: Oxford University Press.

Cabeen, C. W., and Coleman, J. C. (1961). Group therapy with sex offenders: Description and evaluation of group therapy program in an institutional setting. *Journal of Clinical Psychology, 17*, 122–129.

Caplan, H. L., Rohde, P. D., Shapiro, D. A., and Watson, J. P. (1975). Some correlates of repertory grid measures used to study a psychotherapeutic group. *British Journal of Medical Psychology, 48*, 217–226.

Caplan, P. (1995). *They say you're crazy: How the world's most powerful psychiatrists decide who's normal*. New York: Addison-Wesley, Longman.

Carnahan, T. E. (1987) *Rapists' perceptions of women: A repertory grid study*. Unpublished B. A. (honours) thesis, University of Guelph, Canada, April.

Carr, J., and Townes, B. (1975). Interpersonal discrimination as a function of age and psychopathology. *Child Psychiatry and Human Development, 5*, 209–215.

Cautela, J. R. (1966). Treatment of compulsive behavior by covert sensitization. *Psychological Record, 16*, 33–41.

Chambers, W. V. (1985). Measurement error and changes in personal constructs. *Social Behavior and Personality, 13*, 29–32.

Chin-Keung, L. (1988). PCT interpretation of sexual involvement with children. In F. Fransella and L. Thomas (Eds.), *Experimenting with personal construct psychology* (pp. 273–286). London: Routledge and Kegan Paul.

Collings, S. J. (1997). Development, reliability, and validity of the child sexual abuse myth scale. *Journal of Interpersonal Violence, 12*, 665–674.

Cordess, C., and Cox, M. (Eds.) (1996). *Forensic psychotherapy: Crime, psychodynamics, and the offender patient*. London: Jessica Kingsley Publishers.

Craissati, J. (2004). *Managing high risk sex offenders in the community: A psychological approach*. Hove, UK: Brunner-Routledge.

Cullen, E., Jones, L., and Woodward, R. (Eds.) (1997). *Therapeutic communities for offenders*. Chichester, UK: Wiley.

Cummins, P. (2003). Working with anger. In F. Fransella (Ed.), *International handbook of personal construct psychology* (pp. 83–91). Chichester: Wiley.

Darke, J. L. (1990). Sexual aggression: Achieving power through humiliation. In W. L. Marshall, D. R. Laws, and H. E. Barbaree (Eds.), *Handbook of sexual assault* (pp. 55–72). New York: Plenum Press.

Dingman, H. F., Frisbie, L., and Vanasek, F. J. (1968). Erosion of morale in resocialization of pedophiles. *Psychological Reports, 23*, 792–794.

Duck, S. W. (1973). *Personal relationships and personal constructs*. Chichester, UK: Wiley.

Duck, S. W. (1979). The personal and the interpersonal in construct theory: Social and individual aspects of relationships. In P. Stringer and D. Bannister (Eds.), *Constructs of sociality and individuality* (pp. 279–298). London: Academic Press.

Eccles, A., and Walker, W. (2003). Treating offenders in the community: Assessment and treatment issues and the special challenges of sexual offenders. In J. Horley (Ed.), *Personal construct perspectives on forensic psychology* (pp. 143–177). New York: Brunner-Routledge.

Ellis, A. (1962). *Reason and emotion in psychotherapy*. New York: Lyle Stuart.

Ellis, A., and Brancale, R. (1956). *The psychology of sex offenders*. Springfield: Thomas.

Ellis, H. (1933). *Psychology of sex*. London: Heinemann.

Epting, F. R. (1984). *Personal construct counseling and psychotherapy*. New York: Wiley.

Epting, F. R., Gemignani, M., and Cross, M. C. (2003). An audacious adventure: Personal construct counselling and psychotherapy. In F. Fransella (Ed.), *International handbook of personal construct psychology* (pp. 237–245). Chichester, UK: Wiley.

Epting, F. R., Suchman, D. I., and Nickeson, C. J. (1971). An evaluation of elicitation procedures for personal constructs. *British Journal of Psychology, 62*, 513–517.

Epting, F. R., Prichard, S., Leitner, L. M., and Dunnett, G. (1996). Personal constructions of the social. In D. Kalekin-Fishman and B. Walker (Eds.), *The construction of group realities: Culture, society, and personal construct theory* (pp. 309–322). Malabar: Krieger.

Eysenck, H. J. (1964). *Crime and personality*. London: Routledge and Kegan Paul.

Eysenck, H. J. (1977). *Crime and personality* (2nd ed.). London: Routledge and Kegan Paul.

Farran, C. J., Herth, K. A., and Popovich, J. M. (1995). *Hope and hopelessness: Critical clinical constructs.* Thousand Oaks: Sage.

Feixas, G., Molinder, J. L., Montes, J. N., Marie, M. T., and Neimeyer, R. A. (1992). The stability of structural measures derived from repertory grids. *International Journal of Personal Construct Psychology, 5*, 25–39.

Fielding, J. M. (1975). A technique for measuring outcome in group psychotherapy. *British Journal of Medical Psychology, 48*, 189–198.

Finkelhor, D., Hotaling, G., Lewis, I. A., and Smith, C. (1990). Sexual abuse in a national survey of adult men and women: Prevalence, characteristics, and risk factors. *Child Abuse and Neglect, 14*, 19–28.

Fitch, J. L., and Ravlin, E. C. (2005). Willpower and perceived behavioral control: Influences on the intention–behavior relationship and post-behavior attributions. *Social Behavior and Personality, 33*, 105–123.

Forbey, J. D., and Ben-Porath, Y. S. (2002). Use of the MMPI-2 in the treatment of offenders. *International Journal of Offender Therapy and Comparative Criminology, 46*, 308–318.

Foucault, M. (1990). *The history of sexuality: An introduction* (Vol. 1). New York: Vintage Books. (Original work published 1976.)

Frank, J. (1968). The role of hope in psychotherapy. *International Journal of Psychiatry, 5*, 383–395.

Fransella, F. (1968). Self concepts and the stutterer. *British Journal of Psychiatry, 114*, 1531–1535.

Fransella, F., and Adams, B. (1966). An illustration of the use of repertory grid technique in a clinical setting. *British Journal of Social and Clinical Psychology, 5*, 51–62.

Fransella, F., and Bannister, D. (1977). *A manual for repertory grid technique.* London: Academic Press.

Fransella, F., and Joyston-Bechal, M. P. (1971). An investigation of conceptual process and pattern change in a psychotherapy group. *British Journal of Psychiatry, 119*, 199–206.

Fransella, F., Bell, R., and Bannister, D. (2004). *A manual for repertory grid technique.* Chichester, UK: Wiley.

Fraser, M. (1976). *The death of Narcissus.* London: Secker and Warburg.

French, J. R. P., and Raven, B. (1953). The bases of social power. In D. Cartwright and A. Zander (Eds.), *Group dynamics: Research and theory* (pp. 607–623). Evanston: Row, Peterson.

Freshwater, K., Leach, C., and Aldridge, J. (2001). Personal constructs, childhood sexual abuse, and revictimization. *British Journal of Medical Psychology, 74*, 379–397.

Freud, S. (1975). *Three essays on the theory of sexuality.* New York: Basic Books. (Original work published 1905.)

Freund, K. (1990). Courtship disorder. In W. L. Marshall, D. R. Laws, and H. E. Barbaree (Eds.), *Handbook of sexual assault* (pp. 195–208). New York: Plenum Press.

Frisbie, L., Vanasek, F., and Dingman, H. (1967). The self and the ideal self: Methodological study of pedophiles. *Psychological Reports, 20*, 699–706.

Frith, C. D., and Lillie, F. J. (1972). Why does the repertory grid test indicate thought disorder? *British Journal of Social and Clinical Psychology*, *11*, 73–78.

Furby, L., Weinrott, M. R., and Blackshaw, L. (1989). Sex offender recidivism: A review. *Psychological Bulletin*, *105*, 3–30.

Gaines, B. R., and Shaw, M. L. G. (1980). New directions in the analysis and interactive elicitation of personal construct systems. *International Journal of Man–Machine Studies*, *13*, 81–116.

Gendreau, P. (1996). Offender rehabilitation: What we know that needs to be done. *Criminal Justice and Behavior*, *23*, 144–161.

Gendreau, P. (2002). We must do a better job of cumulating knowledge. *Canadian Psychology*, *43*, 205–210.

Giles, P. G., and Rychlak, J. F. (1965). The validity of the role construct repertory grid as a measure of sexual identification. *Journal of Projective Techniques and Personality Assessment*, *29*, 7–11.

Graham, J. R. (2000). *MMPI-2: Assessing personality and psychopathology*. New York: Oxford University Press.

Gray, N. S., Brown, A. S., MacCulloch, M. J., Smith, J., and Snowden, R. J. (2005). An implicit association test of the associations between children and sex in pedophiles. *Journal of Abnormal Psychology*, *114*, 304–308.

Greene, R. L. (1986). The relative efficacy of F-K and the obvious and subtle scales to detect over-reporting of psychopathology on the MMPI. *Journal of Clinical Psychology*, *44*, 152–159.

Greene, R. L. (1997). Assessment of malingering and defensiveness by multiscale personality inventories. In R. Rogers (Ed.), *Clinical assessment of malingering and deception* (pp. 169–207). New York: Guilford Press.

Hagans, C. L., Neimeyer, G. J., and Goodholm, C. R. (2000). The effect of elicitation methods on personal construct differentiation and valence. *Journal of Constructivist Psychology*, *13*, 155–173.

Hanson, R. K., and Morton-Bourgon, K. E. (2005). The characteristics of persistent sexual offenders: A meta-analysis of recidivism studies. *Journal of Consulting and Clinical Psychology*, *73*, 1154–1163.

Hanson, R. K., and Thornton, D. (2000). Improving risk assessments for sex offenders: A comparison of three actuarial scales. *Law and Human Behavior*, *24*, 119–136.

Hare, R. D. (1993). *Without conscience: The disturbing world of the psychopaths among us*. New York: Guilford Press.

Hathaway, S. R., and McKinley, J. C. (1943). *The Minnesota Multiphasic Personality Schedule*. Minneapolis: University of Minnesota Press.

Hayashino, D. S., Wurtele, S. K., and Klebe, K. J. (1995). Child molesters: An examination of cognitive factors. *Journal of Interpersonal Violence*, *10*, 106–116.

Haynes, E. T., and Phillip, J. P. N. (1973). Inconsistency, loose construing, and schizophrenic thought disorder. *British Journal of Psychiatry*, *123*, 209–217.

Helmes, E., and Reddon, J. D. (1993). A perspective on developments in assessing psychopathology: A critical review of the MMPI and MMPI-2. *Psychological Bulletin*, *113*, 453–471.

Hinkle, D. N. (1965). *The change of personal constructs from the viewpoint of a theory of implications*. Unpublished Ph.D. Thesis, Ohio State University, USA.

Holland, R. (1970). George Kelly: Constructive innocent and reluctant existentialist.

In D. Bannister (Ed.), *Perspectives in personal construct theory* (pp. 111–132). London: Academic Press.

Hollin, C. R., and Howells, K. (1991). Sex offenders and victims: The scope of a clinical approach. In C. R. Hollin and K. Howells (Eds.), *Clinical approaches to sex offenders and their victims* (pp. 1–7). New York: Wiley.

Honikman, B. (1973). Personal construct theory and environmental evaluation. In W. F. E. Preiser (Ed.), *Fourth International EDRA Conference* (Vol. 1, pp. 242–253). Stroudsburg: Dowden, Hutchison and Ross.

Honos-Webb, L., and Leitner, L. M. (2001). How using the DSM causes damage: A client's report. *Journal of Humanistic Psychology, 41*, 36–56.

Horley, J. (1987). The units of analysis problem in psychology: An examination and proposed reconciliation. In W. J. Baker, L. P. Mos, H. V. Rappard, and H. J. Stam (Eds.), *Recent trends in theoretical psychology* (pp. 177–187). New York: Springer-Verlag.

Horley, J. (1988a). Cognitions of child sexual abusers. *Journal of Sex Research, 25*, 542–545.

Horley, J. (1988b). The construal of events: Personal constructs versus personal projects. In F. Fransella and L. Thomas (Eds.), *Experimenting with personal construct psychology* (pp. 359–368). London: Routledge and Kegan Paul.

Horley, J. (1991). Values and beliefs as personal constructs. *International Journal of Personal Construct Psychology, 4*, 1–14.

Horley, J. (1992). A longitudinal examination of lifestyles. *Social Indicators Research, 26*, 205–219.

Horley, J. (1995). Cognitive-behavior therapy with an incarcerated exhibitionist. *International Journal of Offender Therapy and Comparative Criminology, 39*, 335–339.

Horley, J. (1996). Content stability in the repertory grid: An examination using a forensic sample. *International Journal of Offender Therapy and Comparative Criminology, 40*, 26–31.

Horley, J. (2000). Cognitions supportive of child molestation. *Aggression and Violent Behavior: A Review Journal, 5*, 551–564.

Horley, J. (2001). Frotteurism: A term in search of an underlying disorder? *Journal of Sexual Aggression, 7*, 51–55.

Horley, J. (2003a). Forensic personal construct psychology: Assessing and treating offenders. In F. Fransella (Ed.), *International handbook of personal construct psychology* (pp. 163–170). Chichester, UK: Wiley.

Horley, J. (2003b). Sexual offenders. In J. Horley (Ed.), *Personal construct perspectives on forensic psychology* (pp. 55–85). New York: Brunner-Routledge.

Horley, J. (2005a). Issues in forensic psychotherapy. In D. Winter and L. Viney (Eds.), *Advances in personal construct psychotherapy* (pp. 250–260). London: Whurr.

Horley, J. (2005b). Fixed-role therapy with multiple paraphilias. *Clinical Case Studies, 4*, 72–80.

Horley, J. (2006). Personal construct psychotherapy: Fixed-role therapy with forensic clients. *Journal of Sexual Aggression, 12*, 53–61.

Horley, J., and Bennett, J. (2003). Psychotherapy with offenders in institutions. In J. Horley (Ed.), *Personal construct perspectives on forensic psychology* (pp. 179–197). New York: Brunner-Routledge.

Horley, J., and Johnson, A. (2008). Meaning and change among domestic abusers.

In J. D. Raskin and S. K. Bridges (Eds.), *Studies in meaning 3: Constructivist psychotherapy in the "real" world* (pp. 127–144). New York: Pace University Press.

Horley, J., and Quinsey, V. L. (1994). Assessing the cognitions of child molesters: Use of the semantic differential with incarcerated offenders. *Journal of Sex Research*, *31*, 187–195.

Horley, J., and Quinsey, V. L. (1995). Child molesters' construal of themselves, other adults, and children. *Journal of Constructivist Psychology*, *8*, 193–211.

Horley, J., and Strickland, L. H. (1984). A note on Jacob Moreno's contributions to the development of social network analysis. *Journal of Community Psychology*, *12*, 291–293.

Horley, J., Carroll, B., and Little, B. R. (1988). A typology of lifestyles. *Social Indicators Research*, *20*, 383–398.

Horley, J., Quinsey, V. L., and Jones, S. (1997). Incarcerated childmolesters' perceptions of themselves and others. *Sexual Abuse: A Journal of Research and Treatment*, *9*, 43–55.

Houston, J. (1998). *Making sense with offenders: Personal constructs, therapy and change*. Chichester, UK: Wiley.

Houston, J. (2003). Mentally disordered offenders. In J. Horley (Ed.), *Personal construct perspectives on forensic psychology* (pp. 87–119). Hove, UK: Brunner-Routledge.

Houston, J., and Adshead, G. (1993). The use of repertory grids to assess change: Application to a sex offenders' group. In N. Clark and G. Stephenson (Eds.), *Sexual offenders: Context, assessment, and treatment. Issues in Criminological and Legal Psychology*, *19*, 43–51.

Howells, K. (1979). Some meanings of children for pedophiles. In M. Cook and G. Wilson (Eds.), *Love and attraction* (pp. 519–526). Oxford: Pergamon.

Howells, K. (1983). Social construing and violent behaviour in mentally abnormal offenders. In J. W. Hinton (Ed.), *Dangerousness: Problems of assessment and prediction* (pp. 114–129). London: Allen and Unwin.

Hucker, S. J., and Bain, J. (1990). Adrogenic hormones and sexual assault. In W. L. Marshall, D. R. Laws, and H. E. Barbaree (Eds.), *Handbook of sexual assault* (pp. 93–102). New York: Plenum Press.

Husain, M. (1983). To what can one apply a construct? In J. Adams-Webber and J. C. Mancuso (Eds.), *Applications of personal construct theory* (pp. 11–28). New York: Academic Press.

Jahoda, M. (1988). The range of convenience of personal construct psychology: An outsider's view. In F. Fransella and L. Thomas (Eds.), *Experimenting with personal construct psychology* (pp. 1–14). London: Routledge and Kegan Paul.

Johnston, L., Hudson, S. J., and Ward, T. (1997). The suppression of sexual thoughts by child molesters: A preliminary study. *Sexual Abuse: A Journal of Research and Treatment*, *9*, 303–319.

Jones, R. E. (1961). Identification in terms of personal constructs: Reconciling a paradox in theory. *Journal of Consulting Psychology*, *25*, 276.

Karp, C., and Rosner, C. (1991). *When justice fails: The David Milgaard story*. Toronto: McClelland and Stewart.

Kelly, G. A. (1955). *The psychology of personal constructs*. New York: Norton.

Kelly, G. A. (1958a). The theory and technique of assessment. *Annual Review of Psychology*, *9*, 323–352.

Kelly, G. A. (1958b). Man's construction of his alternatives. In G. Lindzey (Ed.), *Assessment of human motives* (pp. 33–64). New York: Holt, Rinehart and Winston.

Kelly, G. A. (1963). *A theory of personality*. New York: Norton.

Kelly, G. A. (1969). The role of classification in personality theory. In B. Maher (Ed.), *Clinical psychology and personality: The selected papers of George Kelly* (pp. 289–300). New York: Wiley.

Kelly, G. A. (1970a). A brief introduction to personal construct theory. In D. Bannister (Ed.), *Perspectives in personal construct theory* (pp. 1–29). London: Academic Press.

Kelly, G. A. (1970b). Behavior is an experiment. In D. Bannister (Ed.), *Perspectives in personal construct theory* (pp. 255–269). London: Academic Press.

Kinsey, A. C., Pomeroy, W. B., and Martin, C. E. (1948). *Sexual behavior in the human male*. Philadelphia: Saunders.

Kinsey, A. C., Pomeroy, W. B., Martin, C. E., and Gebhard, P. H. (1953). *Sexual behavior in the human female*. Philadelphia: Saunders.

Kinsman, G. (1991). "Homosexuality" historically considered challenges heterosexual hegemony. *Journal of Historical Sociology*, *4*, 91–111.

Kinsman, G. (1996). *Regulation of desire* (2nd ed.). Toronto: Black Rose Books.

Knight, R. A., Carter, D. L., and Prentky, R. A. (1989). A system for the classification of child molesters: Reliability and application. *Journal of Interpersonal Violence*, *4*, 3–24.

Kong, R., Johnson, H., Beattie, S., and Cardillo, A. (2003). Sexual offences in Canada. *Juristat: Canadian Centre for Justice Statistics*, *23*(6), 1–26.

Krafft-Ebing, R. von (1965). *Psychopathia sexualis*. New York: Special Books. (Original work published 1886.)

Laing, R. D. (1969). *Knots*. Harmondsworth, UK: Penguin.

Landfield, A. W. (1970). High priests, reflexivity, and congruency of client-therapist personal construct systems. *British Journal of Medical Psychology*, *43*, 207–212.

Landfield, A. W. (1971). *Personal construct systems in psychotherapy*. Chicago: Rand McNally.

Landfield, A. W. (1975). The complaint: A confrontation of personal urgency and professional construction. In D. Bannister (Ed.), *Issues and approaches in the psychological therapies* (pp. 2–25). Chichester, UK: Wiley.

Landfield, A. W. (1976). A personal construct approach to suicidal behaviour. In P. Slater (Ed.), *The measurement of intrapersonal space by grid technique. Vol. One: Explorations of intrapersonal space*. Chichester, UK: Wiley.

Landfield, A. W., and Epting, F. R. (1987). *Personal construct psychology: Clinical and personality assessment*. New York: Human Sciences Press.

Langevin, R. (1990). Sexual anomalies and the brain. In W. L. Marshall, D. R. Laws, and H. E. Barbaree (Eds.), *Handbook of sexual assault* (pp.103–114). New York: Plenum.

Lanyon, R. I. (1986). Theory and treatment in child molestation. *Journal of Consulting and Clinical Psychology*, *54*, 176–182.

Laws, D. R. (Ed.) (1989). *Relapse prevention with sex offenders*. New York: Guilford Press.

Laws, D. R., and Marshall, W. L. (1990). A conditioning theory of the etiology and maintenance of deviant sexual preference and behavior. In W. L. Marshall, D. R.

Laws, and H. E. Barbaree (Eds.), *Handbook of sexual assault* (pp. 209–230). New York: Plenum.

Lazarus, A. A. (1971). *Behavior therapy and beyond.* New York: McGraw-Hill.

Lees-Haley, P. R., English, L. T., and Glenn, W. J. (1991) A fake bad scale on the MMPI-2 for personal injury claimants. *Psychological Reports, 66*, 907–911.

Lefebvre, V. A., Lefebvre, V. D., and Adams-Webber, J. (1986). Modeling an experiment on construing self and others. *Journal of Mathematical Psychology, 30,* 317–330.

Leitner, L. M., Begley, E. A., and Faidley, A. J. (1996). Sociality, commonality, individuality, and mutuality: A personal construct approach to non-dominant groups. In D. Kalekin-Fishman and B. Walker (Eds.), *The construction of group realities: Culture, society, and personal construct theory* (pp. 323–340). Malabar: Krieger.

Leman, G. (1970). Words and worlds. In D. Bannister (Ed.), *Perspectives in personal construct theory* (pp. 133–156). London: Academic Press.

Little, B. R. (1972). Psychological man as scientist, humanist and specialist. *Journal of Experimental Research in Personality, 6*, 95–118.

Little, B. R. (1983). Personal projects: A rationale and method for investigation. *Environment and Behavior, 15*, 273–309.

Little, B. R. (1987). Personality and the environment. In D. Stokols and I. Altman (Eds.), *Handbook of environmental psychology* (pp. 205–244). New York: Wiley.

Little, B. R. (2006). Prompt and circumstance: The generative contexts of personal projects analysis. In B. R. Little, K. Salmeia-Aro, and S. Phillips (Eds.), *Personal project pursuit: Goals, actions, and human flourishing* (pp. 3–49). Mahwah, NJ: Lawrence Erlbaum Associates, Inc.

Little, B. R., and Grant, A. M. (2006). The sustainable pursuit of core projects: Retrospect and prospects. In B. R. Little, K. Salmela-Aro, and S. Phillips (Eds.), *Personal project pursuit: Goals, actions, and human flourishing* (pp. 403–444). Mahwah, NJ: Lawrence Erlbaum Associates, Inc.

Lothstein, L. M., and Bach, R. L. (2002). Group therapy with sex offenders. In F. W. Kaslow *et al.* (Eds.), *Comprehensive handbook of psychotherapy: Vol. One* (pp. 501–527). New York: Wiley.

Lutzen, K. (1995). La mise en discours and silences in research on the history of sexuality. In G. P. Parker and J. H. Gagnon (Eds.), *Conceiving sexuality: Approaches to sex research in a postmodern world* (pp. 19–31). London: Routledge.

McCaghy, C. H. (1967). Child molesters: A study of their careers as deviants. In M. Clinnard and R. Quinney (Eds.), *Criminal behavior systems: A typology* (pp. 75–88). New York: Holt, Rinehart, and Winston.

McCaghy, C. H. (1968). Drinking and deviance disavowal: The case of child molesters. *Social Problems, 16*, 43–49.

McCoy, M. M. (1977). A reconstruction of emotion. In D. Bannister (Ed.), *New perspectives in personal construct theory* (pp. 93–124). London: Academic Press.

McCoy, M. M. (1981). Positive and negative emotion: A personal construct theory interpretation. In H. Bonarius, R. Holland, and S. Rosenberg (Eds.), *Personal construct psychology: Recent advances in theory and practice* (pp. 95–104). London: Macmillan.

McCreary, C. P. (1975). Personality differences among child molesters. *Journal of Personality Assessment, 39*, 591–593.

MacCulloch, M. J., Snowden, P. R., Wood, P. J. W., and Mills, H. E. (1983). Sadistic fantasy, sadistic behavior, and offending. *British Journal of Psychiatry, 143,* 20–29.

McPherson, F. M., and Buckley, F. (1970). Thought-process disorder and personal construct subsystems. *British Journal of Social and Clinical Psychology, 9,* 380–381.

McPherson, F. M., Blackburn, I. M., Draffan, J. W., and McFaden, M. (1973). A further study of the grid test of thought disorder. *British Journal of Social and Clinical Psychology, 12,* 420–427.

Mair, J. M. M. (1967). Some problems in repertory grid measurement. I: The use of bipolar constructs. *British Journal of Psychology, 58,* 261–270.

Malamuth, N. M. (1984). Aggression against women: Cultural and individual causes. In N. M. Malamuth and E. Donnerstein (Eds.), *Pornography and sexual aggression* (pp. 19–52). New York: Academic Press.

Marks, I. M., and Sartorius, N. H. (1967). A contribution to the measurement of sexual attitude. *Journal of Nervous and Mental Disease, 145,* 441–451.

Marshall, W. L. (1973). The modification of sexual fantasies: A combined treatment approach to the reduction of deviant sexual behavior. *Behaviour Research and Therapy, 11,* 557–564.

Marshall, W. L. (1996). The sexual offender: Monster, victim, or everyman? *Sexual Abuse: A Journal of Research and Treatment, 8,* 317–335.

Marshall, W. L. (2006). Diagnosing and treating sexual offenders. In I. B. Weiner and A. K. Hess (Eds.), *The handbook of forensic psychology* (pp. 790–818). New York: Wiley.

Marshall, W. L., and Barbaree, H. E. (1988). An outpatient treatment program for child molesters. In R. A. Prentky and V. L. Quinsey (Eds.), *Human sexual aggression: Current perspectives* (pp. 205–214). New York: Annals of the New York Academy of Sciences.

Marshall, W. L., and Barbaree, H. E. (1990). An integrated theory of the etiology of sexual offending. In W. L. Marshall, D. R. Laws, and H. E. Barbaree (Eds.), *Handbook of sexual assault* (pp. 257–278). New York: Plenum Press.

Marshall, W. L., and Mazzucco, A. (1995). Self-esteem and parental attachments of child molesters. *Sexual Abuse: A Journal of Research and Treatment, 7,* 279–285.

Marshall, W. L., Marshall, L. E., Sachdev, S., and Kruger, R.-L. (2003). Distorted attitudes and perceptions, and their relationship with self-esteem and coping in child molesters. *Sexual Abuse: A Journal of Research and Treatment, 15,* 171–181.

Martinson, R. (1974). What works? Questions and answers about prison reform. *The Public Interest, 35,* 22–54.

Masson, J. M. (1984). *The assault on truth: Freud's suppression of the seduction theory.* New York: Farrar, Straus, and Giroux.

Masters, W. H., Johnson, V. E., and Kolodny, R. C. (1988). *Human sexuality.* Glenview: Scott, Foresman.

May, R. (1972). *Power and innocence: A search for the sources of violence.* New York: Norton.

Mead, G. H. (1977). Self. In A. Strauss (Ed.), *George Herbert Mead: On social psychology* (pp. 199–246). Chicago: University of Chicago Press. (Original work published 1934.)

Meehl, P. E. (1954). *Clinical versus statistical prediction: A theoretical analysis and a review of the evidence*. Minneapolis: University of Minnesota.

Meston, C. M., and Buss, D. M. (2007). Why humans have sex. *Archives of Sexual Behavior, 36*, 477–507.

Milan, M. A., Chin, C. E., and Nguyen, Q. X. (1999). Practicing psychology in correctional settings: Assessment, treatment, and substance abuse programs. In A. K. Hess and I. Weiner (Eds.), *The handbook of forensic psychology* (pp. 580–602). New York: Wiley.

Minton, H. L. (1967). Power as a personality construct. In B. A. Maher (Ed.), *Progress in experimental personality research* (Vol. 4, pp. 229–267). New York: Academic Press.

Mischel, T. (1964). Personal constructs, rules, and the logic of clinical activity. *Psychological Review, 71*, 180–192.

Mobley, M. J. (1999). Psychotherapy with criminal offenders. In A. K. Hess and I. Weiner (Eds.), *The handbook of forensic psychology* (pp. 603–639). New York: Wiley.

Mohr, J. W., Turner, R. E., and Jerry, M. B. (1964). *Pedophilia and exhibitionism*. Toronto: University of Toronto Press.

Moreno, J. L. (1978). *Who shall survive? Foundations of sociometry, group psychotherapy, and sociodrama*. Beacon: Beacon House. (Original work published 1934.)

Moulton, H. V., and Marshall, W. L. (2005). Hope in the treatment of sexual offenders: The potential application of hope theory. *Psychology, Crime, and Law, 11*, 329–342.

Needs, A. (1988). Psychological investigation of offending behavior. In F. Fransella and L. Thomas (Eds.), *Experimenting with personal construct psychology* (pp. 493–506). London: Routledge and Kegan Paul.

Neimeyer, R. A. (1985) *The development of personal construct psychology*. Lincoln: University of Nebraska Press.

Neimeyer, R. A., Baker, K. D., and Neimeyer, G. J. (1990). The current status of personal construct psychology. In G. J. Neimeyer and R. A. Neimeyer (Eds.), *Advances in personal construct psychology* (Vol. 1, pp. 3–22). Greenwich: JAI Press.

Neimeyer, G. J., Neimeyer, R. A., Hagans, C. L., and Van Brunt, D.L. (2002). Is there madness in our method?: The effects of repertory grid variations on measures of construct system structure. In R. Neimeyer and G. Neimeyer (Eds.), *Advances in personal construct psychology* (Vol. 5). New York: Praeger.

Nelson, M. C. (1988). Reliability, validity, and cross-cultural comparisons for the simplified Attitudes Toward Women Scale. *Sex Roles, 18*, 289–296.

Ng, S. H. (1980). *The social psychology of power*. London: Academic Press.

Nisbett, R. E., and Wilson, T. D. (1977). Telling more than we can know: Verbal reports on mental processes. *Psychological Review, 84*, 231–259.

Nunes, K. L., Firestone, P., and Baldwin, M. W. (2007). Indirect assessment of cognitions of child sexual abusers with the implicit association test. *Criminal Justice and Behavior, 34*, 454–475.

Orford, J. (1974). Simplistic thinking about other people as a prediction of early drop-out at an alcoholism halfway house. *British Journal of Medical Psychology, 47*, 53–62.

Osgood, C. E., Suci, G. J., and Tannenbaum, P. (1957). *The measurement of meaning*. Urbana: University of Illinois Press.

Palys, T. S., and Little, B. R. (1983). Perceived life satisfaction and the organization of personal project systems. *Journal of Personality and Social Psychology*, *44*, 1221–1230.

Pedersen, F. A. (1958). *Consistency data on the role construct repertory test.* Unpublished manuscript, Ohio State University, Columbus, Ohio, USA.

Peele, S. (1995). *Diseasing of America.* San Francisco: Jossey-Bass.

Prentky, R. A., and Burgess, A. W. (1990). Rehabilitation of child molesters: A cost-benefit analysis. *American Journal of Orthopsychiatry*, *60*, 108–117.

Prentky, R. A., and Knight, R. A. (1991). Identifying critical dimensions for discriminating among rapists. *Journal of Consulting and Clinical Psychology*, *59*, 643–661.

Procter, H., and Parry, G. (1978). Constraint and freedom: The social origin of personal constructs. In F. Fransella (Ed.), *Personal construct psychology* (pp. 157–170). London: Academic Press.

Quinsey, V. L. (1977). The assessment and treatment of child molesters: A review. *Canadian Psychological Review*, *18*, 204–220.

Quinsey, V. L. (1986). Men who have sex with children. In D. N. Weisstub (Ed.), *Law and mental health: International perspectives* (Vol. 2, pp. 140–172). New York: Pergamon.

Quinsey, V. L., and Earls, C. M. (1990). The modification of sexual preferences. In W. L. Marshall, D. R. Laws, and H. E. Barbaree (Eds.), *Handbook of sexual assault* (pp. 279–295). New York: Plenum Press.

Quinsey, V. L., Bergersen, S. G., and Steinman, C. M. (1976). Changes in physiological and verbal responses of child molesters during aversion therapy. *Canadian Journal of Behavioural Science*, *8*, 202–212.

Quinsey, V. L., Harris, G. T., Rice, M. E., and Cormier, C. A. (1998). *Violent offenders: Appraising and managing risk.* Washington: American Psychological Association.

Rada, R. T. (1978). *Clinical aspects of the rapist.* New York: Grune and Stratton.

Radley, A. R. (1974). Schizophrenic thought disorder and the nature of personal constructs. *British Journal of Social and Clinical Psychology*, *13*, 315–327.

Raskin, J. D. (2002). Constructivism in psychology: Personal construct psychology, radical constructivism, and social constructionism. In J. D. Raskin and S. K. Bridges (Eds.), *Studies in meaning: Exploring constructivist psychology* (pp. 1–25). New York: Pace University Press.

Raskin, J. D., and Epting, F. R. (1993). Personal construct theory and the argument against mental illness. *International Journal of Personal Construct Psychology*, *6*, 351–369.

Roberts, J. (1997). History of the therapeutic community. In E. Cullen, L. Jones, and R. Woodward (Eds.), *Therapeutic communities for offenders* (pp. 3–22). Chichester, UK: Wiley.

Roesch, R. (1988). Community psychology and the law. *American Journal of Community Psychology*, *16*, 451–463.

Rogers, R. (1997). Introduction. In R. Rogers (Ed.), *Clinical assessment of malingering and deception* (pp. 1–19). New York: Guilford Press.

Rogers, R., Sewell, K. W., Martin, M. A., and Vitacco, M. J. (2003). Detection of feigned mental disorders: A meta-analysis of the MMPI-2 and malingering. *Assessment*, *10*, 160–177.

Romano, E., and DeLuca, R. (2001). Male sexual abuse: A review of effects, abuse characteristics, and links with later psychological functioning. *Aggression and Violent Behavior, 6*, 55–78.

Rowe, D. (1971). An examination of a psychiatrist's predictions of a patient's constructs. *British Journal of Psychiatry, 118*, 231–244.

Rowe, D. (1994). *Wanting everything: The art of happiness*. London: HarperCollins.

Ryle, A., and Breen, D. (1972). A comparison of adjusted and maladjusted couples using the double dyad grid. *British Journal of Medical Psychology, 45*, 375–382.

Ryle, A., and Lunghi, M. (1969). The measurement of relevant change after psychotherapy: Use of repertory grid testing. *British Journal of Psychiatry, 115*, 1297–1304.

Ryle, A., and Lunghi, M. (1970). The dyad grid: A modification of repertory grid technique. *British Journal of Psychiatry, 117*, 323–327.

Ryle, A., and Lunghi, M. A. (1971). A therapist's prediction of a patient's dyad grid. *British Journal of Psychiatry, 118*, 555–560.

Salter, A. C. (1988). *Treating child sex offenders and victims: A practical guide*. Beverly Hills: Sage.

Salter, A. C. (2003). *Predators: Pedophiles, rapists, and other sex offenders*. New York: Basic Books.

Sartre, J.-P. (1956). *Being and nothingness: An essay in ontology*. New York: Liveright.

Schneider, J., Bosley, J. T., Ferguson, G., and Main, M. (2006). The challenges of sexual offense treatment programs in correctional facilities. *Journal of Psychiatry and Law, 34*, 169–196.

Segal, Z. V., and Stermac, L. E. (1990). The role of cognition in sexual assault. In W. L. Marshall, D. R. Laws, and H. E. Barbaree (Eds.), *Handbook of sexual assault* (pp. 161–176). New York: Plenum Press.

Sewell, K. W., and Saleron, R. T. (1997). Understanding and detecting dissimulation in sex offenders. In R. Rogers (Ed.), *Clinical assessment of malingering and deception* (pp. 328–350). New York: Guilford Press.

Shapiro, D. A., Caplan, H. L., Rohde, P. D., and Watson, J. P. (1975). Personal questionnaire changes and their correlates in a psychotherapeutic group. *British Journal of Medical Psychology, 48*, 207–216.

Shorts, I. D. (1985). Treatment of a sex offender in a maximum security forensic hospital: Detecting changes in personality and interpersonal construing. *International Journal of Offender Therapy and Comparative Criminology, 29*, 237–250.

Shotter, J. (1970). Men, the man-makers: George Kelly and the psychology of personal constructs. In D. Bannister (Ed.), *Perspectives in personal construct theory* (pp. 223–253). London: Academic Press.

Silverman, I. (1983). *Pure types are rare*. New York: Praeger.

Skene, R. A. (1973). Construct shift in the treatment of a case of homosexuality. *British Journal of Medical Psychology, 46*, 287–292.

Slater, P. (1969). Theory and technique of the repertory grid. *British Journal of Psychiatry, 115*, 1287–1296.

Smail, D. J. (1970). Neurotic symptoms, personality and personal constructs. *British Journal of Psychiatry, 117*, 645–648.

Space, L. G., and Cromwell, R. L. (1980). Personal constructs among depressed patients. *Journal of Nervous and Mental Disease, 168*, 150–158.

Space, L. G., Dingemans, P. M., and Cromwell, R. L. (1983). Self-construing and alienation in depressives, schizophrenics, and normals. In J. Adams-Webber and J. C. Mancuso (Eds.), *Applications of personal construct theory* (pp. 365–377). New York: Academic Press.

Sperlinger, D. J. (1976). Aspects of stability in the repertory grid. *British Journal of Medical Psychology, 49*, 341–347.

Stam, H. J. (1990). Rebuilding the ship at sea: The historical and theoretical problems of constructivist epistemologies in psychology. *Canadian Psychology, 31*, 239–253.

Stermac, L. E., and Segal, Z. V. (1989). Adult sexual contact with children: An examination of cognitive factors. *Behavior Therapy, 20*, 573–584.

Stermac, L. E., Segal, Z. V., and Gillis, R. (1989). Social and cultural factors in sexual assault. In W. L. Marshall, D. R. Laws, and H. E. Barbaree (Eds.), *Handbook of sexual assault* (pp. 143–159). New York: Plenum Press.

Strachan, A., and Jones, D. (1982). Changes in identification during adolescence: A personal construct theory approach. *Journal of Personality Assessment, 46*, 529–535.

Stringer, P. (1979). Individuals, roles, and persons. In P. Stringer and D. Bannister (Eds.), *Constructs of sociality and individuality* (pp. 91–114). London: Academic Press.

Taylor, L. (1972). The significance and interpretation of replies to motivational questions: The case of the sex offender. *Sociology, 6*, 24–39.

Varble, D. L., and Landfield, A. W. (1969). Validity of the self-ideal discrepancy as a criterion measure for success in psychotherapy: A replication. *Journal of Counseling Psychology, 16*, 150–156.

Viney, L. L., Metcalfe, C., and Winter, D. A. (2005). The effectiveness of personal construct psychotherapy: A meta-analysis. In D. Winter and L. Viney (Eds.), *Personal construct psychotherapy: Advances in theory, practice, and research* (pp. 347–364). London: Whurr.

Walters, G. D. (1990). *The criminal lifestyle: Patterns of serious criminal conduct.* Newbury Park: Sage.

Walters, G. D. (2000). *Beyond behavior: Construction of an overarching psychological theory of lifestyles.* Westport: Praeger.

Walters, G. D. (2005). Mapping the criminal mind: Idiographic assessment of criminal belief systems. *International Journal of Offender Therapy and Comparative Criminology, 49*, 5–24.

Ward, T., and Gannon, T. (2006). Rehabilitation, etiology, and self-regulation: The Good Lives Model of sexual offender treatment. *Aggression and Violent Behavior, 11*, 77–94.

Ward, T., Hudson, S. M., and France, K. G. (1993). Self-reported reasons for offending behavior in child molesters. *Annals of Sex Research, 6*, 139–148.

Ward, T., Hudson, S. M., and Marshall, W. L. (1994). The abstinance violation effect in child molesters. *Behavior Research and Therapy, 32*, 431–437.

Ward, T., Hudson, S. M., and Marshall, W. L. (1995a). Cognitive and affective deficits in sexual aggression: A cognitive deconstructionist analysis. *Sexual Abuse: A Journal of Research and Treatment, 7*, 67–83.

Ward, T., McCormack, J., and Hudson, S. M. (1997b). Sexual offenders perceptions of their intimate relationships. *Sexual Abuse: A Journal of Research and Treatment, 9*, 57–74.

Ward, T., Hudson, S. M., Johnston, L., and Marshall, W. L. (1997a). Cognitive distortions in sex offenders: An integrative review. *Clinical Psychology Review, 17,* 479–507.

Ward, T., Louden, K., Hudson, S. M., and Marshall, W. L. (1995b). A descriptive model of the offense chain for child molesters. *Journal of Interpersonal Violence, 10,* 452–472.

Warr, P. B. (1971). Pollyanna's personal judgments. *European Journal of Social Psychology, 1,* 327–338.

Warren, W. (1998). *Philosophical dimensions of personal construct psychology.* London: Routledge.

Watson, J. P. (1970a). A measure of therapist-patient understanding. *British Journal of Psychiatry, 117,* 319–321.

Watson, J. P. (1970b). A repertory grid method of studying groups. *British Journal of Psychiatry, 117,* 309–318.

Watson, J. P. (1972). A possible measure of change during group psychotherapy. *British Journal of Medical Psychology, 45,* 71–77.

Weber, M. (1964). *The theory of social and economic organization.* New York: Free Press. (Original work published 1947.)

Weeks, J. (1995). History, desires, and identities. In G. P. Parker and J. H. Gagnon (Eds.), *Conceiving sexuality: Approaches to sex research in a postmodern world* (pp. 33–50). London: Routledge.

Weigel, R. G., Weigel, V. M., and Richardson, F. C. (1973). Congruence of spouses' and reported marital success: Pitfalls in instrumentation. *Psychological Reports, 33,* 212–214.

Willutzki, U., and Duda, L. (1996). The social construction of powerfulness and powerlessness. In D. Kalekin-Fishman and B. Walker (Eds.), *The construction of group realities: Culture, society, and personal construct theory* (pp. 341–361). Malabar: Krieger.

Wilson, G. D., and Cox, D. N. (1983a). Personality of paedophile club members. *Personality and Individual Differences, 4,* 323–329.

Wilson, G. D., and Cox, D. N. (1983b). *The child-lovers: A study of paedophiles in society.* London: Peter Owen.

Winter, D. A. (1988). Reconstructing an erection and elaborating ejaculation: Personal construct theory perspectives on sex therapy. *International Journal of Personal Construct Psychology, 1,* 42–53.

Winter, D. A. (1992a). *Personal construct psychology in clinical practice: Theory, research and applications.* London: Routledge.

Winter, D. A. (1992b). Repertory grid technique as a group therapy research instrument. *Group Analysis, 25,* 449–463.

Winter, D. A. (2003a). The evidence base for personal construct psychotherapy. In F. Fransella (Ed.), *International handbook of personal construct psychology* (pp. 265–272). Chichester, UK: Wiley.

Winter, D. A. (2003b). A credulous approach to violence and homicide. In J. Horley (Ed.), *Personal construct perspectives on forensic psychology* (pp. 15–54). New York: Brunner-Routledge.

Winter, D. A. (2005). Towards a personal construct sex therapy. In D. Winter and L. Viney (Eds.), *Advances in personal construct psychotherapy* (pp. 287–295). London: Whurr.

Winter, D. A. (2007). Construing the construction processes of serial killers and other violent offenders: The limits of credulity. *Journal of Constructivist Psychology, 20,* 247–275.

Winter, D. A., and Viney, L. L. (Eds.) (2005). *Personal construct psychotherapy: Advances in theory, practice, and research.* London: Whurr.

Winter, D. A., and Watson, S. (1999). Personal construct psychotherapy and the cognitive therapies: Different in theory but can they be differentiated in practice? *Journal of Constructivist Psychology, 12,* 1–22.

Wrong, D. (1979). *Power: Its forms, bases, and uses.* New York: Harper and Row.

Yorke, M. (1989). The intolerable wrestle: Words, numbers, and meanings. *International Journal of Personal Construct Psychology, 6,* 65–76.

Name index

Subject index